The Black Nation Novel

THE BLACK NATION NOVEL

Imagining Homeplaces in Early African American Literature

Adenike Marie Davidson

Third World Press, Chicago

Third World Press
Publishers since 1967
Chicago

First Edition
Printed in the United States of America

Cover design by Keir Thirus

Library of Congress Cataloging-in-Publication Data
Davidson, Adenike Marie.
 The Black nation novel: imaginging homeplaces in early African American literature/Adenike Marie Davidson.—1st ed.
       p. cm.
  Includes bibliographical references.
  ISBN-13: 978-0-88378-281-1 (alk. paper)
  ISBN-10: 0-88378-281-2 (alk. paper)
1. American fiction—African American authors—History and criticism.
2. Black nationalism in literature. 3. African Americans in literature.
4. Politics and literature—United States—History—19th century. I. Title.
  PS374.N4D38 2007
  813'.409358—dc22

                                              2007036653
12 11 10 09 08 07   6 5 4 3 2 1

For Brenda, Clive, and Zenzile

Many thanks to—

My family for their love and support always; my girlfriends for their humor in the tough times; my colleagues and friends for acting as sounding boards, long talks and advice; Fisk University (colleagues, administrators, and students) for giving me an academic and nurturing homeplace; and Third World Press for their encouragement, patience, and support in seeing this through, and most importantly, giving this project a homeplace.

CONTENTS

Black Nationalism and the Freedom of the Novel

Black nationalism, as it has been conceived by the popular contemporary imagination, is often reactionary and militant, but perhaps a more important recent phenomenon, it's usually misinterpreted by outsiders as a sort of hatred of whiteness. The words of Toni Morrison's character, Guitar, of the Seven Days Group in *Song of Solomon* explains—"What I'm doing ain't about hating white people. It's about loving us. About loving you. My whole life is love" (160). Examining what I have termed "Black nation novels"—novels written by African Americans that expressly imagine a Black nation as an autonomous and nurturing space and reject the quest for inclusion into America—I acknowledge a tradition that is long standing and has historical resonance with contemporary Black nationalist political and literary movements.

My work is influenced by three theories that frame the concepts of nationalism, Black nationalism, and the novel as a site of nation building. First, Karl Marx's definition of nation as a community having a common language, territory, economic life and perspective is the starting ground for any discussion of nation building.[1] Second, working beyond this definition in an attempt to expand and concretize the idea of nation, Kenneth Minogue, in *Nationalism* (1967), suggests that nationalism, and the movement towards nation formation, "is a political movement depending on a feeling of grievance against foreigners" (Minogue 25). And third, Ernest Renan, in "What is a nation?" (1882), concludes, "A nation is a spiritual principle, the outcome of the profound complications of history; it is a spiritual family not a group determined by the shape of the earth" (Renan 18-19). Black nationalism, frequently dismissed by white scholars as specious because it seems to deviate in various ways from conventional definitions of nationalism, nevertheless has many points of congruence with the definitions of nationalism in Marx, Minogue, and Renan.[2] For instance, Marx defines territory as a prerequisite for nationhood, yet Black nationalism does not always assume a particular physical location. One aspect of white supremacy in the United States is, indeed, a preventing by force the possibility for Black Americans to control territory. A lack of access to sovereign land does not negate the issue of territory, however, and as we will see again and again in the pages that follow, Black nationalism often includes a "quest for territory" as a means of solidifying nationhood and gaining the power necessary to resist, rebuff, or otherwise survive white aggression.

Another way in which Black nationalism resonates with conventional nationalist theory is in the importance it places on religion and spirituality. Returning to Renan's emphasis on spirituality as an aspect of nation, and the nation as a spiritual family, we can recognize in Black nationalism the thread of Ethiopianism, an ideology that sprang out of shared political and religious experiences of English-speaking Africans during the late eighteenth and early nineteenth centuries. Ethiopianism weaves itself throughout these texts, particularly the novels by Delany and Hopkins. The name of the movement is derived from the Biblical scripture Psalm 68:31: "Princes shall come out of Egypt; Ethiopia shall soon stretch forth her hands unto God." This verse was interpreted by some as a prophecy that Africa would "soon" be saved from the darkness of heathenism, and as a promise of dramatic political,

2

industrial, and economic renaissance. Others insisted that the real meaning of the scripture is that some day the Black man would rule the world, thus reversing white supremacy. Ethiopianism, then, is more than a vague allusion to Ethiopia, but a call for world revolution and universal elevation of the status of African peoples. As Africans in the New World converted to Christianity, they found Biblical paradigms and prophecies for interpreting Black experiences in the nineteenth century; these helped fuel abolitionist movements in the antebellum period and later looked toward a more positive future and a Pan-Africanist interpretation of the connection of all people of African descent as "Ethiopians" and heirs in the redemption of Africa. In Ethiopia, African Americans found images of themselves,[3] a glorious past,[4] proof of a history other than heathenism and savagery,[5] and most important a promise for a revived future through Psalm 68:31. This verse aided in the notion of racial uplift because it demonstrated that rather than God having cursed Africans and those of African descent, as those claimed who promoted the Hamatic myth, that instead God promised to guide African advancement.

While nineteenth century interpretations of this Biblical reference differed widely, the main themes that emerged were that Ethiopia was a symbol for all Africans, that God had prophesied the redemption of Africa, and that the mission of those of African descent was to work towards this redemption. Ethiopianism asserted that Africans, although historically devalued by whites, would eventually rise to greatness. It was important for African Americans to reclaim a civilized past in order to refute charges of inherent African inferiority promoted through Social Darwinism. The redemption of Africa would parallel the redemption of those of African descent, debased through their scattering from the homeland and the shame of New World slavery. In an attempt to connect their present condition of oppression and the Biblical promise of greatness, many African Americans connected their history to the Christian idea of the "fortunate fall." This ideology attempted to explain the experience of slavery as a positive and necessary step in a Divine plan. In *The Negro Problem and the Method of Its Solution* (1891), R.C.O. Benjamin, an African American minister, asserts that:

> Slavery was a providential rock in the building of God's plan for the redemption of Africa. ...there is no other solution of the Negro problem than the general enlightenment of the Negro in the country, preparatory to taking his position as the morning star of Africa's regeneration. (19-20)

Still Wilson Jeremiah Moses, in *The Wings of Ethiopia* (1990), explains that "the impulse towards the uplifting of the Black American masses was never too far removed from the vision of African regeneration" (96). Thus, African Americans, enlightened by Christianity, assumed that they would return to Africa and revive the civilization which was debased by its adoption of idolatry so long ago.[6]

Between 1877 and 1900, independent Black churches sponsored missionaries of their own in Africa. Casely Hayford, in *Ethiopia Unbound* (1911), explains "Ethiopianism developed in those parts of the world with invidious racist antinomy" (xxiii), and "Ethiopia became a metaphysical Black heaven, ...emblematic of African valour and resistance" (xxiv, xxvi). Ethiopianism included an attempt to stop white missionaries from destroying African values, a belief that Africa belonged to Africans, and an opposition to European interference. This missionary, or messianic destiny, rested primarily on African Americans. In *Black Messiah and Uncle Toms* (1982), Wilson Jeremiah Moses claims the "Black messianism is a very American tradition" (5), and he identifies four different varieties of messianic phenomena found in African American literature: the expectation or identification of a personal savior; racial messianism, a concept of the redemptive mission of the Black race; messianic symbolism; and "prophetism" and "prophetic movements" (1). It is through Black messianism that these authors imagine a Black nation.

One basis for dismissing Black nationalism as a deviation from conventional nationalist theory is its foregrounding of race and its dependence on race as a unifying aspect of Black nation formation, regardless of language, economic life and perspective. Although race is absent in Marx's definition, we may see race (especially whiteness) as a fundamental issue in the defining and building of the United States as a nation. The exclusion of Native and African Americans from citizenship and the relatively speedy inclusion of European immigrants, despite differences in language, religion, ethnic identity and even class, suggests that race can be very important to nation formation.[7] The conclusion that race is inextricably linked to nationalism could be reinforced with comparisons to other New World cases, though, strictly speaking, such comparisons lie outside the scope of the present study. In the late nineteenth century, Cuba, Brazil, and Argentina all employed so-called "whitening" policies that encouraged the wholesale emigration and immediate incorporation of European migrants in order to counteract the perceived threat of a free Black population.[8]

Such examples help make a convincing case that New World perspectives generally include race as a determining factor for nation formation, and since we are specifically concerned with Black nationalism as a New World phenomenon, it seems reasonable to expect that blackness, as well as whiteness, could serve as a determinant of nation formation. Minogue's argument that nations must have "grievances against foreigners" can be adapted as another way of understanding how Black nationalism poses race as a unifying national experience. In this analogy, African Americans are united in grievance against the pretensions of white supremacy and the depredations of white-on-black violence, and shared oppression based on race is a basic commonality.

5

Renan's reference to spirituality, and his definition of the nation as a "spiritual family," also bears upon our understanding of Black nationalism in three ways. First, it helps to understand the inclusion of liberation theology in Black nation ideology, especially Ethiopianism and the universal elevation of the status of African people based on Biblical scripture. Second, it supports the examination of how Black nationalism resonates with more conventional notions of nationalism, even though Black nationalism does not always include territory as a primary condition. Third, focusing on spirituality encourages the defining of blackness, and the history of oppression, as positive aspects of shared cultural production, instead of simply negative experiences of shared oppression.

While it is helpful to point out where Black nationalism resonates with conventional nationalist theory, we also need to take stock of the uniqueness of Black nationalism, and of efforts to theorize it on its own terms. Most often defined as the belief that people of African descent living in the New World constitute a nation, Black nationalism is usually associated with 1960s political thought and action, though often traced as well to the 1920s with Marcus Garvey's back-to-Africa movement. The history of Black nationalist theory and practice has a much longer history in North American, however. E.U. Essien-Udom, in *Black Nationalism* (1962), defines this movement as "the belief of a group that it shares, or ought to share, a common heritage of language, culture, and religion; and that its heritage, way of life and ethnic identity are distinct from those of other groups ... [and] that [this group] ought to rule themselves and shape their own destinies" (Essien-Udom 20). Here Essien-Udom includes the importance of religion but also adds the political desire for self-determination which suggests separation from a larger political body. As early as the late 1700s, sections of the African American community saw themselves as separate from the larger nation—not simply as a reaction to political exclusion—and

6

sought to separate as a means of determining their own futures. In 1787, eighty African Americans from Boston petitioned the state legislature for funds to pay for their passage to and to buy land in Africa, explaining that they wanted to leave because their circumstances were "very disagreeable and disadvantageous" (Quarles 96). In that same year, the Free African Society was founded in Philadelphia and proposed the return of Africans to Africa. Separatist projects in the antebellum era included organized migration efforts to Liberia, Sierra Leone, Canada, and Haiti. After the Civil War separatist energies focused on westward migration by the so-called Exodusters and various groups seeking to form Black utopian communities in Oklahoma, Kansas, and Nebraska. In the 1880s, Martin Delany expressed renewed interest in African migration as a supporter of the Liberian Exodus Joint Stock Steamship Company.[9]

Keeping in mind Marx's emphasis on "shared territory" as a paradigmatic aspect of nationhood, we can begin to specify the uniqueness of Black nation building in the United States with a recognition that a discrepancy exists between North American territory as a "birthplace" and North America as a problematic "homeplace" for people of African descent. The possibility for Black people to experience North American territory as a space where they might feel complete and productive remains an elusive goal despite the fact that North America has been the birthplace for people of African descent for nearly four hundred years. These centuries of existence on North American soil notwithstanding, the challenge remains of how, in the words of Toni Morrison, "to convert a racist house into a race-specific yet non-racist home" (Morrison, "Home" 8). Homeplace as an aspect of nationhood might be further specified, then, as territory in which one feels complete and productive. For people of African descent, homeplace would mean a space in which blackness might be experienced as a positive form of political empowerment and not as a mark of estrangement and alienation. bell hooks captures some of the political resonance I have in mind for the concept of homeplace when she argues that "loving blackness as political resistance transforms our ways of looking and being, and thus creates the conditions necessary for us to move against the forces of domination and death and reclaim black life" (hooks, *Black Looks* 32). Homeplace is a space defined by the act of loving blackness, and within which loving blackness becomes possible.

Resolving the discrepancy between birthplace and homeplace is a comprehensive, long term project that defines the political, economic, and cultural contours of Black nation-building. Viewed as a matter of politics, the pursuit of homeplace has entailed diverse strategies including covert resistance, civil disobedience, and litigation to secure civil rights, and even forms of insurrection not motivated by desperation and vengeance but by the desire to achieve autonomy. Politically, the movement toward collective action and securing a homeplace as a form of protection against white supremacist violence is the ultimate goal of nation building for people of African descent.

The most important strategy for recreating the United States as a homeplace has been racial uplift, a form of activism practiced by the elite segment of the African American community during the nineteenth century. Racial uplift was widely adopted after Emancipation and promoted especially through the Black church. Its purpose was to enable the masses educationally, financially, and spiritually to battle and overcome racism and racial oppression. With each individual success came a responsibility to help another in the community reach success; the goal was that thereby racial prejudice would be systematically dismantled, African Americans would prove themselves as productive and contributing citizens, and America would live up to its ideal as a democratic nation, as the sweet land of liberty. Proponents of racial uplift believed in the viability of this plan because not because it was considered "white," but because its characteristic values were widely accepted, respected and understood as civilized. Because the enslavement of Africans had been justified by Europeans as a "civilizing mission," the adoption of racial uplift was seen as an opportunity to prove to the dominant society that the African American community was civilized and therefore worthy of and deserving of equality and opportunities.

Kevin Gaines, in *Uplifting the Race* (1996), explains that racial uplift was "an ideology of class differentiation, self-help, and interdependence in the hope that unsympathetic whites would relent and recognize the humanity of middle-class African Americans and their potential for citizenship rights" (3). Its goal was to assist the process of African Americans becoming as conventionally American as possible with the expectation of being rewarded with inclusion—citizenship and professional success. The negative aspect of racial uplift was the responsibility it placed on the African American community, especially those of the working and lower classes, to change those characteristics seen as weaknesses, brought on by slavery, but interpreted as inherently racial. This eager acceptance of dominant society's interpretation of the community, and the desire to change in order to be accepted by the dominant society, is the fatal flaw to racial uplift ideology— unconscious internalized racism. I examine the ways in which these authors critique racial uplift as a viable strategy for the preferred goal of inclusion into the nation. Through this critique, the authors grapple with the larger question of whether to have faith in the United States as a possible future homeplace or to seek emigration to some other location where the major foundation of a homeplace—the inclusion and valuing of blackness—might be more attainable.

I examine definitions and representations of the changing Black nation found in a series of early African American novels that, as a group, form what I refer to as the

"Black nation novel." Martin Delany's *Blake; or, The Huts of America* (1859), Sutton Griggs's *Imperium in Imperio* (1899), Pauline Hopkins's *Of One Blood; or, The Hidden Self* (1902), and W.E.B. Du Bois's *The Quest of the Silver Fleece* (1911) and *Dark Princess: A Romance* (1928) are all texts that use the novel to configure varied Black collectivities within and without the United States. Rejecting dominant models of assimilation conveyed in canonical American and in much African American literature, these authors maintain both that the African American community is connected to a larger international community and that it has the basis for forming its own nation within the larger American community. While individual texts typically place more emphasis on either domestic or global approaches to nation building, one of the distinctive qualities of the genre as a whole is that Black nation novels encompass both ideas. Although the idea and possible reality of a Black nation is theorized by Delany, Griggs, Hopkins, Du Bois, and other authors of political nonfiction between 1850 and 1930, what becomes most important in my project are the ways in which these writers move from theoretical speculation to the depiction of concrete "imagined communities" in their works. The novels I have chosen to examine attest to the freedom fiction allows the imagination in creating communities, and regathering the materials of the world into a newly-envisioned moral order. As it is essential for African Americans to speak for themselves politically, so too do these authors and texts attest that it is equally important for the community to imagine, desire and execute their own creative destiny.

Fictional representations of Black nationalism or Black nation novels are important documents for determining the evolution of thinking about the formation of a Black nation. Creating an imagined homeplace is a cultural as well as a political endeavor and it is against this larger backdrop of cultural struggle for freedom that the specific cultural work of the Black nation novel becomes comprehensible.

Structural aspects of the genre, i.e., its characteristic thematic and narrative devices, need to be understood as tools of articulation that advance the process of reimagining and redefining birthplace as homeplace. While the idea of homeplace may be founded on the political goal of securing territory, these novels clarify and define crucial qualitative settings and conditions that help concretize an African American homeplace as a fuller, more easily imagined reality.

Many literary critics have engaged in a parallel examination of the novel as a literary form and as representative of the onset of nationalism. The argument is compelling that the novel, a site of comparatively greater ideological freedom, has been a significant constitutive tool of nation building. Ian Watt, in *The Rise of the Novel* (1964), asserts that "[p]revious literary forms had reflected the general tendency of their cultures to make conformity to traditional practice the major test of truth. . . . This literary traditionalism was first and most fully challenged by the novel, whose primary criterion was truth to individual experience" (Watt 13). The notion that novels provide greater scope for free expression takes on special resonance when applied to early African American fiction. The desire to achieve freedom, both physical (of the body) and spiritual (of the voice as the essence of the soul), and to define the racialized body and self, is evident in much early African American literature. Moreover, early African American fiction became and remains an excellent medium for removing the racialized self from the auction block while preserving the religious, political, and social customs of the community. Fiction, for early Black writers, becomes a substitute commodity for the Black body. Black nation novels, I would argue, go even further by expanding the discursive range within the field of African American culture, even as that field is being formed. Just as Watt concludes that the novel gives expression to the changing political environment in England in the eighteenth century, the Black nation novel challenges traditional strategies of racial uplift and the desire for inclusion in white America by the African American community.

M.M. Bakhtin, in *The Dialogic Imagination* (1981), defines the novel as "a diversity of social speech types...and a diversity of individual voices, artistically organized" (263). Bakhtin's concept of diverse social speech types applies in two ways to the Black nation novel. Viewed in comparatively narrow terms, as an aspect of the genre, we can readily identify the clash and interplay of Black voices that reflect a range of class positions, political ideologies, regional experiences, philosophical and religious codes, written and oral verbal traditions, and so on. All of this typifies the dialogic energy that for Bakhtin is characteristic of all novels. At a somewhat more general level of analysis, study of the Black nation novel reveals a greater sense of the diversity of social speech types within African American literature as a whole. Bringing Black nation novels to the center of our inquiry reveals ideas, beliefs, desires, and agendas typically not associated with the characteristic "uplift" of early African American novels. Imagining a Black nation as separate from the United States complicates assumed notions about African American voice and thought based on studies of canonical African American novels, such as William Wells Brown's *Clotel* (1854), Charles Chesnutt's *The House Behind the Cedars* (1900), or Nella Larsen's *Passing* (1929). Particularly unsettled by a sustained reading of Black nation novels is the assumption that the desire and quest for inclusion is normative. This subversive quality of the Black nation novel, its ability to call traditional canons of thought and taste into question, exemplifies the central principle of Bakhtin's theory of the novel, and we can see how subversion applies in striking ways even when the scope of analysis is focused on tradition and counter-tradition within African American cultural history.

The visions of Black nations found in Black nation novels fit with what Benedict Anderson, in *Imagined*

Communities (1983), called "the imagined community," in which "in the minds of each [member] lives the image of communion" (Anderson 6). In these novels, characters come to a consensus regarding the community of a Black nation and strive towards that formation. Anderson sees the nation (both real and fictional) as "an imagined political community . . . inherently limited and sovereign" (Anderson 6). Defining the nation as "imagined," Anderson allows us to look seriously at the Black nation in these novels. The Black nation novel challenges conventional notions of the United States as a melting pot, a diverse and inclusive entity, and a land of democracy and freedom. Homi Bhabha, in "DissemNation," asserts that "counternarratives of nation that continually evoke and erase its totalizing boundaries— both actual and conceptual—disturb those ideological maneuvers through which 'imagined communities' are given essentialist identities" (Bhabha). The Black nation novel, as a counternarrative of nation, reflects what Watt calls "innovating reorientation" (Watt 20); it attempts to reorient the African American community's identification with North America as the desirable homeplace and with Africa as the land of heritage but not as a desirable home in the present.

While these theories help to understand the narrative structure of Black nation formation, Black nation novels require us to revise Marx, Anderson, and Bhabha to account for the unique contours of African American nationalist discourse. First, because they reflect the experience of an oppressed "nation" without a homeland, the fictions in this study contain quests for territory (rather than assuming territory as Marx imagines). Second, they introduce the idea of diaspora as a collectivity that challenges Anderson's understandingof nation. While diaspora does not depend on the idea of "sovereign territory," it is, generally speaking, inherently limited to people of a specific descent, in this case African. Third, while Black nation novels recognize that there is no official language in the diaspora, they engage in a

13

consistent effort to reclaim a collective culture, both national and global, with historical roots.

This diaspora, the dispersal of people of African descent across several continents, is not technically a territory with established boundaries but the acceptance of shared heritage and the understanding of white supremacy as a danger to people of color everywhere. It creates a type of political territory; this political territory is not "inherently limited" to people of African descent, but inclusive of all people of color who are of similar political consciousness. Thus I have adopted Anderson's claim that imagined communities "are to be distinguished, not by their falsity/genuineness, but by the style in which they are imagined" (6). The novels in this study cross several genres—picaresque, speculative fiction, utopia, and romance—as the authors attempted to present an alternative reality with which their readers were already familiar and sometimes even comfortable, thereby projecting a transformed world, a social revolution and/or a radical change in the depiction of reality.

As Black nationalists, these authors are working with a collective assumption and definition of the necessary components of a Black nation (whether inside or outside North America): a traditional family structure in which marriage is valued, the wife is protected sexually and physically, and the husband is able to provide financially; a spirituality which nurtures but also supports action rather than contentment; and an environment which allows for ambition and the development of one's mind—all of this may be interpreted as racial uplift, but racial uplift that includes no dependence on whites or conformity to white values. Throughout this study, three thematic concerns emerge as central, recurrent topics: spirituality, family life, and the problem of whether or not to seek inclusion in the dominant social order. The authors in this study move away from inclusion which would mean the devaluing of blackness, and move towards valuing and centering blackness. They construct sites striving towards an achievable, modern utopia, with an imagined Ethiopia as the spiritual and political model.

In articulating these thematic concerns, practitioners of the Black nation novel employ certain distinctive narrative devices. Many of these devices are reflective of the novel and its subgenres. The authors in this study use general aspects of novelistic discourse, particularly the capacity of the novel—noted by Bakhtin, Watt, Anderson, and others—in an effort to redeploy heterogeneous social content such as political, religious, artistic, and other speech forms for the purposes of national identity formation. In individual chapters, I will comment on the compliance or noncompliance of Black nation novelists with generic formulas, and the meaning that such formulas assume in the context of Black nation-building.

There is one important narrative device that deserves special mention as it is characteristic of all these texts, and indeed helps us to conceptualize the Black nation novel as a distinctive subgenre with its own internal dynamic of authorial influence, and its own pattern of audience address. I refer here to the pattern of narrative call-and-response, which I establish and trace among these authors and texts. By call-and-response, I mean the African American cultural art form that fosters and reinforces a dynamic relationship between individual and community, between generations, between literature and folk culture, and between the quest for justice and the struggle against racial oppression. Most simply, these texts are responses to the dominant society's calls for exclusion of blackness as evidenced in racist legislation and physical violence visited upon Black bodies. More important to this study though, is Robert Stepto's adaptation of call-and-response to explain an internal dynamic within African American literature. In *From Behind the Veil* (1979), Stepto frames the interplay of freedom and literacy as a dialectical coupling that functions as a literary form of call-and-response. He writes, "freedom

15

occasions literacy and literacy initiates freedom" (3). While Stepto limits his examination of the narrative process to canonical texts within an African American literary tradition, I suggest that the pattern applies—in a unique way—to the less-familiar tradition of Black nation novels. If we allow for the possibility of expanding the scope of call-and-response as Stepto defines it, we can easily see how this device might also be applied to the particular thematics of Black nation novels. For example, the search for homeplace, initiated by the questioning of racial uplift ideology, occasions the Black nation novel, which in turn intensifies the search to define and realize a homeplace.

A "call" may be as simple as a questioning of the status quo, such as Frederick Douglass's "What to the Slave is the Fourth of July?" and Sojourner Truth's "Ain't I A Woman?," or as complicated as a "call for action," such as David Walker's *Appeal* (1829). But a "call" presupposes a specific listening audience and expects a response of some sort. A "response" requires more than the call. Stepto asserts that "a response is fundamentally an artistic art of closure performed upon a formal unit that already possesses substantial coherence. There can be no one response, no one and final closure; there can only be appropriate responses, and what is appropriate is defined by the prefiguring call that has come before." A "response" assumes no time limit on the call and also the authority to participate in the dialogue. Although the authors in this study are all responding to the same original calls—Ethiopianism and uplift—as the society changes tactics for exclusion, so too must the responses change their tactics. The responses in this study address the domestic/global dichotomy, whether to stay in North America or find some suitable place to emigrate and build a nation, faced by the African American community, and their attempt to imagine and resolve this split. Also, each response then becomes a call for the next generation. Finally, because audience determines the pattern of call-and-response dynamics, it is also important to relate the concept of audience to the fictional texts I examine. Delany's and Hopkins's novels were both published in serial form in African American periodicals. Griggs's novel was self-published and sold door-to-door. Only Du Bois's novels were originally released through a publishing house, indicative of some gains in inclusion over the years. Thus we assume a predominantly Black audience for all except Du Bois.

My study is structured chronologically and recognizes and considers the legal, political, and cultural changes within the United States that affect and influence the strategies adopted by the African American community for survival. In each of the chapters I give particular attention to the ideological dimensions of inclusion and exclusion that these novels explore, primarily from a masculine point of view.[10] I link this masculine quest for inclusion in the dominant United States national community to the quest for nationhood. I theorize that imagining nationhood as a masculine quest allowed opportunities to prove "Black manhood" and expose the multilayered attempts at emasculation within the domestic nation plot. I then discuss how the domestic nation plot disempowers the Black man as well as the Black woman. A move towards imagining Black community as a global diasporic entity allows for a greater autonomy in Black manhood and opens the door to active participation by Black women in the task of collective empowerment.

Chapter one examines the antebellum period, 1830-1860, a time of extreme uncertainty and hostility for all African Americans. Historical obstacles included racial slavery, the passing of anti-black laws (the 1850 Fugitive Slave law and the 1857 Dred Scot Decision), an increased sense of hopelessness, and the search for new plans. While the majority of African Americans were committed to remaining in the United States and hopeful for future abolishment of slavery and inclusion of productive African Americans, a small minority retained a more pessimistic outlook of the possibility of future inclusion and called for emigration to some foreign territory that looked upon "blackness" as a welcoming sign instead of a mark of inferiority. Martin Delany's novel, *Blake; or, The Huts of America* (1859), provides the nascene to which the following authors respond, and this chapter examines Delany's ideology of Black nationalism and the movement of African American fiction in the direction of global horizons. Delany's life reflects numerous splits in African American strategies. His ideas often conflicted with those of other race leaders of his time, especially Frederick Douglass. Delany battled all of his adult life with the question of whether to remain in the states or to emigrate elsewhere. As a free born African American, Delany is representative of that elite class who seem to be most affected by this inner conflict regarding the quest for inclusion. Delany's only novel, *Blake*, establishes for this study the major issues addressed by the authors following him. After publishing several non-fiction political pieces, Delany turned to the novel in an attempt to capitalize on the influence of fiction that he saw in Harriet Beecher Stowe's *Uncle Tom's Cabin* (1852). In the novel, he imagines issues previously addressed in print only through nonfiction: mass emigration, Christianity as detrimental to Black autonomy, the need for unity among people of African descent within the diaspora, and the reclaiming of Black manhood and womanhood.

Delany's *Blake*, the first Black nation novel, provides the template to which subsequent texts in the genre adhere. Set in antebellum America and Cuba, *Blake* is divided into two parts. The first examines the futility of believing in inclusion and a domestic nation, while the second explores the possibility of a global entity—the organizing of Africans, Afro-Caribbeans, and African Americans for territorial, political, and financial success. This division of the novel into domestic and global spheres illustrates the divided strategic path the African American community has faced (as long as the domestic nation remains hostile to the inclusion of blackness). Because the plot of Delany's novel is shrouded in secrecy (a trope repeated in all of the novels of this study) and ends without resolutions (neither domestic nor global), I view it as a call to the African American antebellum community, the next generation of race leaders, and new authors imagining the Black nation. The novel also serves as a response to the antebellum calls of David Walker, Henry Highland Garnet, Robert Alexander Young, and Alexander Crummell for autonomous action and a coalition of all African peoples.

Chapter two begins with an examination of the turn of the twentieth century as a time of great turbulence, agitation and instability for African Americans. The end of slavery and the experiment of Reconstruction created renewed hope in the possibility of inclusion and, interestingly, we find during this period a hiatus in the production of Black nation novels questioning inclusion along the lines explored in Delany's *Blake*. But the end of Reconstruction, the founding of the Ku Klux Klan, its increasing strength, and the establishment of Jim Crow laws forced African Americans to reconsider former plans of separation or of establishing all-Black communities out West. During this era, also known as the "the nadir," African Americans produced new fictional responses to the antebellum calls for Black nation formation and the return of Black nation novels. Using Sutton Griggs's first novel, *Imperium in Imperio* (1899), as the central text, I examine in this chapter the beginnings of "New Negro" and racial uplift ideology as political strategies in the quest for inclusion, and acknowledge Delany and the antebellum period as precursors to racial uplift. Griggs, a Baptist minister, follows Delany in using the novel as a powerful tool for enacting change, self-publishing five novels and selling them door-to-door within the Black community. *Imperium* is a direct response to Delany's concept of "a nation within a nation." Griggs "responds" to several issues "called" by Delany: the potential for Black solidarity to be compromised through color and class differences, the emasculation of Black manhood within the domestic nation, and the necessity for secrecy in developing and nurturing Black autonomy. But unlike Delany who quickly establishes the futility in the quest for inclusion, due to antebellum reality, Griggs's novel examines in detail the development of the New Negro through racial uplift strategies as a means of securing inclusion. Also unlike Delany, Griggs remains committed to a domestic nation plot but examines a separate Black territory within the domestic nation as a possible solution. In his imagining, Griggs further develops Delany's declaration of the Black family as the cornerstone to the Black nation, as well as argues that a domestic nation solution is a dangerous threat to the Black family. Griggs is unable to imagine a successful configuration of the Black family on domestic soil, something Delany is able to envision only outside of a domestic territory. This inability of both Delany and Griggs establishes a pattern (and call) taken up as a challenge by the last two authors in this study. I conclude that the domestic nation plot is conducive in a limited way to the reclaiming and empowerment of Black manhood, but the global plot allows the imagining of Black male and female partnership/leadership and thus the empowerment of Black female autonomy and the inclusion of all African Americans in the imagined community.

Chapter three continues the examination of the turn of the twentieth century with the increasing racist activity in America as well as America's increasing imperialist goals. For African Americans, awareness of international affairs was also shaped by Ethiopia's defeat of Italy at the end of the nineteenth century. This event brought the image of Ethiopia as a great Black nation back into the forefront of African American consciousness. Using Pauline Hopkins's *Of One Blood* (1902) and W.E.B. Du Bois's *The Souls of Black Folk* (1903) as the central texts, I examine in this chapter the continued critique of racial uplift as a viable strategy for domestic inclusion. Hopkins, through the use of "Talented

Tenth" characters, quickly establishes that the quest for inclusion is futile. Her characters find inclusion only through passing which suggests that the only means of success lies in a negation and devaluing of blackness. Hopkins then follows Delany's second path, seeking a global, rather than a domestic, entity. She locates this global community within the ideal Black nation of Ethiopia and examines the African American's connection outside of the birthland. Hopkins cannot envision a satisfying domestic community and sees in it only a replication of racial and gender hierarchy and the horrors of the antebellum plantation system, including rape and murder. Instead, Hopkins's global solution imagines a revitalized Black family as leading the progress of the community towards Black autonomy. She ends her novel with a royal marriage and acknowledges Black motherhood as a vital component of the Black nation. Hopkins's global plot is a response to the inability of Delany and Griggs to imagine the full inclusion of Black womanhood as essential to race leadership, and a call to the next generation of race leaders and Black nation novel authors to further extend the possibility of Black male and female partnership.

Chapter four moves from the turn of the twentieth century to pre-Harlem Renaissance, examining W.E.B. Du Bois's *The Souls of Black Folk* (1903) and his first novel, *The Quest of the Silver Fleece* (1911). Once again, I examine the necessity of using the novel as a tool for creating political changes through Du Bois's move into the realm of fiction. The novel allows Du Bois to be more provocative in exploring solutions to the problem of the color line not available to him in the genre of nonfiction and political prose because of the danger he saw in Booker T. Washington's program of accommodation and industrial education. In this chapter, I begin by examining Du Bois's commitment to the goal of inclusion in the domestic nation, evident in his racial uplift and Talented Tenth strategies. Although he does not consider a global configuration at the time of *The Quest of the Silver Fleece* he does re-examine in that work the limits of racial uplift. In particular, he suggests that uplift entails disconnection from the masses, a devaluing of the skills and talents of the folk, and a flawed concept of leadership by the Talented Tenth. This reexamination in turn also questions the purpose, possibility, and rewards (if any) of inclusion. Thus Du Bois explores Delany's first path, the development of Black nationhood domestically and the quest for inclusion through racial uplift. He also further extends Griggs's conception of a separate domestic territory. But unlike Delany and Griggs, Du Bois incorporates Black womanhood and leadership into his sense of community and responds to Hopkins's call for leadership based on partnership between Black men and women. Du Bois also distinguishes the differences between the New Negro and the Talented Tenth, as well as the effects and purposes of each: the former comes out of the folk and leads the masses, while the latter is seen as apart from the folk but useful in the struggle to break down racial prejudice in the dominant society. Du Bois acknowledges disappointment in the quest for inclusion but is unable to imagine healing the class rift in the African American community. He ends the novel with a presentation of the Black woman as better qualified for Black nation leadership.

Chapter five examines the Harlem Renaissance period and the hope of Black intellectuals that the positive reception of African American literature could achieve blocked political goals. In the early twentieth century as the United States and European countries strengthened their positions as empires through the colonization of African and Caribbean countries, the States also increased its blatant exclusion of African Americans from full citizenship and the nation. Using Du Bois's second novel, *Dark Princess: A Romance,* as the central text, I examine in this chapter his turn to a global solution, which includes a critique of the quest for inclusion into the domestic nation, and the imagination of Black autonomy as dependent upon the coalition of African Americans with colonial peoples seeking national liberation. Irish nationalism, India's struggle for independence, Du Bois's Pan-African movement, combined with the Red Summer of 1919 and increased racial violence, caused Du Bois to revisit global solutions. In this novel, Du Bois reconciles many of the issues that he grappled with in his own nonfiction, as well as those issues addressed previously in Black nation novels by the authors in this study.

In *Dark Princess*, Du Bois returns to Delany's template by first critiquing the possibility of a domestic solution. But he also extends Delany's call for a global entity by defining and connecting the struggles of Asian peoples to those of the African diaspora against white supremacy. Du Bois also extends Griggs's critique and examination of racial uplift by explicitly exploring the need for grassroots organization and work by the "Talented Tenth" leadership in order to achieve effectiveness. Finally, Du Bois answers fully the call of Hopkins for an acknowledgment of the necessity of partnership between Black men and women in the forming of the nation. Extending his own representation of Black women as equal race leaders, which he explored in *Quest*, Du Bois ends *Dark Princess* with a complete imagining of the healthy and productive racial home. The novel ends with a loving couple, committed to self-determination and the fight against white supremacy, producing an heir for the future, who represents a messianic child; a resolution not found in any of the previous texts.

The novels in this study provide evidence of an important though neglected tendency in the African American novel tradition. Typically that tradition is seen as inclusion oriented, especially as one examines the desires of African American authors to appeal to a white audience as a means of persuasion and change. Militant, separatist, and global ideas are commonly believed to originate in the 1960s, or as early as the Harlem Renaissance with Marcus

Garvey's Back to Africa movement. The study shows the much larger history of a minor, but vocal, authorial presence in African American literature wrestling with issues of inclusion but finding them futile and looking towards means of separation, both domestic and global.

CHAPTER ONE

Martin R. Delany Issues the Call and Sets the Template with *Blake; or, The Huts of America*

We must make an issue, create an event, and establish a national position for ourselves.

—Martin R. Delany

Geography, teaches a knowledge of the world, and political economy, a knowledge of the wealth of nations. . . These are not abstruse sciences, or learning not easily acquired or understood; but simply, common School primer learning, that every schoolboy may get. And, although it is the very Key to propensity and success in common life, but few know anything about it.

—Martin R. Delany

Frederick Douglass, in his 1852 speech, "What to the Slave is the Fourth of July?" explains, "I am not included within the pale of this glorious anniversary! Your high independence only reveals the immeasurable distance between us" (Douglass 385). Douglass's concern focused on the African American masses left behind in the South suffering in the peculiar institution of which he had first-hand knowledge. But by the mid-nineteenth century, it was painfully clear that the African American, whether enslaved

25

or free, would not be included in the foundation of independence, opportunity and democracy of the nation. The continuation and commitment to racial slavery, the passing of anti-Black laws, and the increased support of the American Colonization Society's desires to remove free African Americans from North American soil all contributed to an increased sense of hopeless. But despite blatant exclusion, many African Americans were vested in making the United States a home, having no real memory of Africa as a homeland and living in the land of their birth.

Douglass's vocalization of the position in which African Americans found themselves, excluded from full participation in their "native" land, is a response to dominant society's refusal to acknowledge the humanity of African Americans and to the abolitionist community's passive resistance to the nation's continued practice of slavery. But his statement can also be taken as a call to the African American community for a plan of action that bridges the distance he presents; this call is followed by two different responses from African American race leaders and novelists—emigration, integration and/or assimilation. Martin R. Delany, race leader, medical doctor, and former business partner of Douglass, was a very vocal minority voice for emigration. This chapter presents Delany's only novel as the foundation for the tradition of the Black nation novel. It is through him that the idea of a separate Black nation led by African Americans is first articulated and fictionalized. This articulation comes during a turbulent and unstable political period before the Civil War. Delany's importance also lies in his use of the novel to imagine the Black nation; as a writer of several nonfiction pieces, we see through his only novel, the imaginative and political freedom that comes with the genre.

Although slave narratives were widely used by abolitionists as proof of the humanity of African Americans and the inhumane treatment suffered in bondage, the validity of authorship and of facts presented in the texts was often questioned. The success of Harriet Beecher Stowe's novel, *Uncle Tom's Cabin*, proved fiction to be a more persuasive political tool. Eight texts from this period before the Civil War mark a move by African American writers away from writing autobiography, slave and spiritual narratives and toward writing fiction: Victor Sejour's "The Mulatto" (1837), William Wells Brown's *Clotel; or, The President's Daughter* (1853), Frederick Douglass's *The Heroic Slave* (1853), Frank Webb's *The Garies and Their Friends* (1857), Frances Ellen Watkins Harper's "The Two Offers" (1859), Martin R. Delany's *Blake; or, The Huts of America* (1859)[1], Harriet E. Wilson's *Our 'Nig'; or Sketches from the Life of a Free Black, In a Two-Story White House, North. Showing That Slavery's Shadows Fall Even There* (1859), and Harriet Ann Jacobs's *Incidents in the Life of a Slave Girl* (1861). Except the recently discovered short story by Sejour, all appear after the success of Stowe's *Uncle Tom's Cabin*. William Andrews, in "The Novelization of Voice in African American Narrative," explains that "[b]y the early nineteenth century Black narrators realized that to assume the privileged status of author in the literary discourse of white America, they would have to write self-authorizing, that is, self-authenticating, narratives" (23).

While these texts address racial oppression in the United States, during such an unstable era, as Carla Peterson asserts in *Doers of the Word*, "these novelized texts offered alternative worlds that, unlike history or autobiography, permitted an elaboration of the future and the representation of endings of African American life-stories" (149). It is within this context that Delany turns towards fiction, and specifically the novel, to explore the political goals he actively but ultimately unsuccessfully worked towards fulfilling.

Delany's only attempt at a novel, *Blake; or, The Huts of America*, is considered the most radical African American novel of the nineteenth century "in characterization and theme" (Bell 51). Delany follows his literary contemporaries in his abolitionist theme, expanding on the structure of the slave narrative, and examining financial independence as a means towards combatting racism and oppression. But Delany's novel diverts from the templates of other antebellum African American fiction through the use of a full Black protagonist, a blatant disregard for a white audience, a willingness to abandon "Christianity" and Christian ethics, a move away from presenting either the North (including Canada) or Europe as a haven by centering freedom in the Caribbean, and by presenting the possibility and necessity of Pan-African unification against white supremacy.

Of the five early Black nation novels in this study, Delany's *Blake* has received the greatest amount of attention from literary critics during the last thirty years. This interest stems from Floyd Miller's reprint of the novel in 1970, from the establishment of African American studies programs in many academic institutions, and from the examination of the history of Black nationalism in the United States, both products of the Civil Rights Movements of the 1960s. In this environment, *Blake* becomes an important text in helping to understand the move from slave narrative to fictive narrative in the African American literary tradition.[2] For the purposes of this study *Blake* is seen as the first Black Nationalist novel, and the first "Black Nation Novel."

Most of the literary criticism on Delany's novel falls into one or more of the following camps. Literary historians consider *Blake* important based on its antebellum publication but accord the novel very little literary merit. Psychoanalytic critics approach the text as Delany's fantasy of violence against whites. Sociopolitical critics consider *Blake* as Delany's attempt to authenticate himself as a race leader, and as a fictive treatment of the political issues faced by African Americans in antebellum America. In the first camp, critics acknowledge that *Blake* does not follow a neat template, but instead mixes genres of slave narrative, picaresque, and romance, which Floyd Miller concludes, in his "Introduction" to the novel, brings "a much more complex (and truthful) rendering of mid-nineteenth century black experience" (xxi). Because of the missing final chapters, the overall unity is considered to be somewhat compromised. Miller sees the ending as a benefit to twentieth century readers, and states that "the very inconclusiveness of the novel as it now exists—the rebellion in process—is perhaps more relevant today than any ending Delany could possibly have conceived" (xxv). While the novel is accredited with portraying a militant Black leader, a figure suppressed in other texts, most critics find *Blake* lacking as a novel. Jean Fagan Yellin, in *The Intricate Knot* (1972), reduces the novel to "a revolutionary handbook outlining the organization of a guerrilla army of Black liberationists" (199).

Other critics have chosen to focus on the novel as a fantasy of Delany's desires, namely racial violence against white America. In psychoanalytical readings of the text, the protagonist Blake is seen as an extension of the author Delany, and the motivations and desires of Blake as Delany's projections and wish fulfillment of his own life. Ronald Takaki, in *Violence in the Black Imagination* (1972), argues that "Revolutionary violence, even the violence happening in the fantasy of fiction, offered Delany a means to free himself from the anguish of ambivalence he felt toward America and Africa and affirm clearly and simply his blackness and his identity with the land of his ancestry" (99). Although certainly different in tone than the other antebellum fictive narratives, *Blake* (in the form available to us today) is actually not very bloody. And similar to Douglass's *The Heroic Slave*, most of the Black on white violence is talked about but not shown. What is made explicit in *Blake*, is the white on Black violence, both physical and emotional. Similar to Sejour's "The Mulatto," Blake's revolutionary action stems from the removal of his wife at the hands of the slave master, which symbolizes for him his exclusion from humanity. To see *Blake* as an exceptionally violent text for its time period is to concentrate only on the absence of revolutionary violence in other early African American texts and to assume a white audience for Delany's novel as should be assumed for the other antebellum novels. The African American antebellum fictive narratives, such as *Clotel* and *Incidents in the Life of a Slave Girl*, have an obvious white readership in mind that accounts for the use of "near-white" characters and themes of Black suffering and Black desire for integration. Considering a largely Black audience for *Blake* explains the absence of pandering to white thought and the focus on Black self-help and self-determination.

Blake is also interpreted as the working out of Delany's political strategies for Black empowerment (emigration, freemasonry, and civilization) in fictive form. In *Resistance and Reformation* (1995), John Ernest believes that "Delany creates a fictive community of unified black revolutionaries in order to change a more incoherent and fragmented reality" (17), and also "*Blake*, fiction though it may be, is Delany's own practical application of principles adduced; the novel is 'the thing carried out'" (114). Critics that fall into this camp also see *Blake* as a fictive response to the political and literary climate of the time, the increase in political disenfranchisement and the promotion of passive Black male characters. In *To Wake the Nations* (1993), Eric Sundquist concludes that "[c]alling for the exercise of black revolutionary force, Delany replied to [Harriet Beecher] Stowe, Douglass, and conceivably to [Herman] Melville [*Benito Cerino*] in *Blake*" (183).

Lastly, *Blake* is viewed as the text written by Delany in an attempt to authenticate him as a race leader. This need to authenticate himself stems from Frederick Douglass's position as head spokesman, ex-slave, promoter of integration, and author of a well-received slave narrative. Delany on the other hand, free born and a defender of emigration, was a minority political voice. Robert Levine, in

Martin Delany/Frederick Douglass (1997), concludes that "Delany presents in *Blake* a Pan-African vision of black nationalism that means to combat and expose the limits of the US nationalism espoused by blacks aligned with Douglass" (190). In both cases—as a blueprint for Black empowerment and as a self-authenticating claim for race leadership—sociopolitical critics treat the literary text as a mirror reflecting the political agenda of the author.

While I see the importance of examining *Blake* as one of the foundational pieces in the African American literary tradition, I think it's more pertinent to establish the text as the building block for the Black nation novel in African American literature. Whereas others see *Blake* as a deficient text for exploring the development of a tradition, I find the text, with its domestic and global plots, especially vital in establishing the dichotomous nature of the Black nation novel. Although I agree with the sociopolitical importance critics place on the novel's exchange with the political challenges of the time, I see, its importance in a cultural context as well. Certainly Delany is responding to the political exclusion and literary stereotyping of African Americans, but I believe he is also critiquing culturally-based strategies of empowerment adopted by the African American community—racial uplift, civilization, and spirituality. Without an awareness of this cultural horizon, traditional psychoanalytical readings appear limited in scope. Instead of assuming racism and white supremacy as Delany's motivations for revolutionary action, a mostly reactionary reading of Black self-determination, I examine the novel through its position of rejecting the dominant African American aspirations to inclusion. When examined in this way, actions of violence, spirituality, and racial uplift are less in response to political exclusion and more connected to the forming of a national community, the determining of the best means for survival and success, and the self-defining of blackness as a positive manifestation of the community.

Delany was no stranger to the influential power of literature, having edited two African American newspapers, and by 1859 already having published three books and authored "The Political Destiny of the Colored Race," and been witness to the success of several slave narratives as well as the extreme popularity of Harriet Beecher Stowe's *Uncle Tom's Cabin* (1850).[3] Thus Delany entered the powerful world of fiction, along with a handful of other African American antebellum authors, seeing the novel as a new tool for creating community and regathering "the material of the world into a newly imagined order" (Ernest 112).

The novel begins with the tribulation of Blake and his wife, Maggie, two enslaved African Americans considered by dominant society as different from and of higher status than the masses of slaves. Both are highly intelligent, moral, and, as a marker of their elite status, speak standard English instead of the dialect of the slaves. Their separation entitles them to certain privileges not available to the masses—finer clothes, literacy, and the opportunity to hire out their time and skills. These advantages create a false sense of inclusion for Maggie and Blake, making them comfortable and unwilling to disturb the status quo. Such an examination by Delany is a critique of the role of the free African American in antebellum America, who enjoyed certain privileges, albeit limited, while their brethren suffered as slaves. For Delany, the Fugitive Slave Law of 1850 made clear that any partial inclusion is false and tenuous. Blake and Maggie must also come to a similar conclusion. Therefore the first half of the novel explores the ways in which the quest for inclusion into the American nation is futile, and that such a quest jeopardizes the stability of the Black family and demands allegiance to a false sense of spirituality. Blake and Maggie come to understand their actual exclusion, despite appearances, when Colonel Franks abruptly sells her very near the beginning of the novel.

Black Women and Domestic Nation Building

Delany chooses to introduce the reader to his "heroine" before his "hero." Repeating the pattern of much antebellum African American fiction, Maggie is a mulatta and quite beautiful. She is introduced in relation to the plantation mistress, and the reader is told, "The conduct of Mrs. Franks toward her servant was more like, that of an elder sister than a mistress, and the mistress and maid sometimes wore dresses cut from the same cloth" (6). Maggie is not the average slave woman and Mrs. Franks is far from the typical plantation mistress. Her presentation as a darker Mrs. Franks is a construction not of immoral slave but of true woman.[4] This image is reinforced when we are told, "Maggie was true to her womanhood, and loyal to her mistress" (8), suggesting that Maggie subscribes to the same values found in dominant society. For this "crime"—valuing her womanhood and her purity—she is suddenly sold and separated from her husband and child.[5]

Maggie's absence becomes the motivating catalyst for her husband's rebellious nature. When an unjust authority breaks the stability of his family structure, Blake suddenly sees clearly the immoral institution of slavery. He decides that he can no longer be a willing or even silent participant in his own oppression and suddenly finds his voice, which threatens the hierarchy of oppression. He tells the other slaves, "I'll never call him 'master' again, except when compelled to do so" (18). Moreover, Blake attributes his rebellion against oppressive conditions to his wife's absence, and expresses this to Franks while defiantly refusing to obey orders: "When I last rode that horse in company with your and [your] lady, my wife was at my side, and I will not go without her!" (19). Such blatant insubordination compels Franks to make an example of Blake, and he threatens the rebellious man with being placed on the auction block and even being killed.

Blake views his marriage to Maggie, while living in a society which excludes blackness and compels him on a quest for inclusion, as an entanglement that prevents greater personal success. This "burden" can be viewed two ways. In the more literal sense, the married Black man is distracted away from "nation" concerns through the focus on personal success represented in the family structure. Thus nation-building can only occur without the burden and responsibility of a family. In the North American setting which involves the quest for inclusion, the focus and energy that would be used for nation-building is transferred onto keeping the home and Black womanhood, protected from the same dominant society into which the African American desires inclusion and therefore an entanglement. Once Maggie is removed, her absence breaks the illusion of inclusion as well as the burden of protection and Blake can focus on community progress and success.

The other way this entanglement may be interpreted includes viewing Blake's love of Maggie as symbolic of the love of the African American for his or her birthland. Maggie's absence is akin to abandonment (although no fault of her own), since she leaves without saying goodbye and Blake expects a welcome from her when he returns from his outing for Franks. Maggie does not fulfill her obligation as wife, and America does not fulfill its obligation as homeland to the African American. Colonel Franks comes between Blake and Maggie with the authority (as slave owner dealing with his property) to redefine and restructure their relationship. Although they are "married," Franks does not respect their union and feels justified in both expecting Maggie to submit to his sexual desires and in breaking up the Black family for financial gain. Paralleling this, the government separates the African American from the nation by perverting the ideals of democracy and excluding the African American from citizenship and human status. Blake does not in turn abandon Maggie, but is reunited with her later in the novel away from an authority committed to their separation. Similarly, Blake and his comrades seek to be reunited with the ideal of home away from authorities committed to the exclusion of blackness.

Because of Maggie's sudden absence, the reader is never shown the racial home of the partially included Black family; perhaps Delany wishes to reinforce the idea that there is no such possibility that is safe and productive in antebellum America. The racial home of Maggie and Blake in the first half of the novel, while not yet ideal, is an improvement on the home of Mammy Judy and Daddy Joe. The masses of enslaved African Americans in the novel must be convinced of their desire and ability to be free, and Maggie and Blake already possess such an understanding, although they have not acted upon the desire. Maggie, unlike Mammy Judy, upholds the ideal of an unsullied womanhood, which in turn supports Blake's manhood in several ways. Upon his return, Blake's first inquiry regarding Maggie's absence is, "Is Maggie dead?" (15). After reassurance that she is not, he questions "Has she disgraced herself?" (15). Mammy Judy's response reveals the survival skills by which she lives but which are unproductive for the Black family. She tells Blake, "No chile, may be better she dun so, den she bin heah now an' not sole. Maus Stephen sell eh case she!—I dun'o, reckon dats da reason" (15). First, knowing that Maggie is committed to resisting white male lust at all costs, even at the cost of being sold or even killed—a commitment that Blake proposes to other slave women on his conversion travels— allows him to concentrate on other avenues of resistance. Because he knows that Franks has not succeeded in stealing Maggie's purity, and was therefore forced to remove her to show his power and control, Blake in turn does not feel belittled but is instead empowered. This presentation of Blake contrasts sharply with the presentation of Daddy Joe who is shown as emasculated and comical.

As Delany presents it, unsullied womanhood allows for a true patriarchal home with the Black male in a position of power, there being no questions about the paternity of the family offspring. Franks, as white patriarch and father of Maggie, is empowered to rule his "home" as he sees fit. This includes his slaves and his slave daughter, Maggie. In similar fashion, Blake feels empowered to also manage his "home" and removes the remainder of his family, his son and in-laws, from the Franks plantation to "free" soil in Canada. As the Black home and family becomes the possible only space of "freedom"—in the novel there is a continual search for a locale that values blackness—Maggie's purity strengthens this space as a foundation for political action in the pursuits of other freedoms. Her refusal to submit to sexual impurity is seen as political resistance that in turn encourages and demands defiance from Blake. While Delany presents men as responsible for any necessary physical action in an insurrection, the Black woman's main priority in the insurrection is to keep her womanhood pure, even at the cost of life.

Spirituality and Domestic Nation Building

In addition to critiquing the idea of a safe and productive racial home is possible within the domestic nation, due to racial exclusion and the dominant society's commitment to weakening this foundation in the African American community, Delany also critiques the adoption of Christianity in its passive form as a step toward possible future inclusion. In response to Maggie's absence, Blake refuses to pray and instead lashes out against the hypocrisy of Christianity that African Americans have been told to adopt:

> Don't tell me about religion! What's religion to me? My wife is sold away from me by a man who is one of the leading members of the very church to which she and I belong! Put my trust in the Lord! I have done so all my life nearly, and of what use is it to me? My wife is sold from me just the same as if I didn't. (16)

Blake's anti-religion speech introduces three very important points concerning spirituality. First, it seems counterproductive to Black self-determination to subscribe to a religion similar to that of one's oppressors, unless one is resigned to a position of subservience. Franks, as a leading member of the church, exposes the duplicity of Christianity, which is simply being used by Franks and his class as a foundation for American slavery. Second, Blake suggests the need for a spirituality that does something and produces results. From the slaveholder's point of view, Christianity was useful in that it provided justification of their actions and it pacified the enslaved to seek a reward in the afterlife instead of on earth. Blake surmises that a sense of empowerment should come from the spirituality of African Americans. Delany is not willing to whole-heartedly reject Christianity, for to do so would put his main character in danger of being labeled as a heathen or a savage. He takes great pains to present Blake in the light of the educated, and has Blake justify his critique of religion to those who question his rejection of prayer: "I do trust in the Lord as much as ever, but I know I understand him better than I used to, that's all. I don't intend to be made a fool of any longer by false preaching" (20). Here Delany critiques the messenger instead of the message. He knows that dominant society desires for the African American community to accept inferior status, and promotes such a viewpoint through Christianity.

Finally, Blake makes clear to the reader and to fellow Blacks that his sense of spirituality must have some usefulness to the conditions of life:

> You must make your religion subserve your interests, as your oppressors do theirs! . . . They use the Scriptures to make you submit, by preaching to you the texts of 'obedience to your masters' and 'standing still to see the salvation,' and we must now begin to understand the Bible so as to make it of interest to us. (41)

Blake defines religion as a form of homeplace in which the change of perspective is allowed; a comfortable spirituality which grows with one's worldly experience rather than a stifling religion which repeats the same solutions for new and ever changing problems.

Unlike the immoral slaveholder with his sense of spirituality, Blake does not attempt to claim a position of religious authority, although the rest of the slave community sees him as a messiah figure. His refusal to be seen as spiritual leader is directly tied to his commitment to action as well as prayer:

> I am not fit, brother, for a spiritual leader; my warfare is not Heavenly, but earthly; I have not to do with angels, but with men; not with righteousness, but wickedness. Call upon some brother who has more of the grace of God than I. If I ever were a Christian, slavery has made me a sinner; if I had been an angel, it would have made me a devil! I feel more like cursing than praying—may God forgive me! Pray for me, brethren! (103)

While the reader is shown Blake's humble nature first hand, we cannot help but to compare his honesty here with Delany's previous critique of Colonel Franks's involvement of the church with his own immoral acts.

After critiquing the weakened position of the Black family and the adoption of a counterproductive spirituality within the domestic sphere while pursuing the quest for inclusion, Delany proposes that no domestic Black nation will succeed without a radical reformation of Black thought and action. We have already noted that this revolution must include Black female resistance to rape and the adoption of a useful spirituality. The majority of part one of the novel explores the third component of this necessary radical reformation—a secret plan. Blake spends time covertly educating select slaves, usually men, on several plantations throughout the South. At his first secret meeting, he states, "I have laid a scheme, and matured a plan for a general insurrection of the slaves in every state, and the successful overthrow of slavery!" (39). Blake recognizes as a priority the need to awaken slaves to their own humanity and potential, which has been dormant for generations due to their enslaved condition. Once Blake "awakens" the slaves, as he has been awakened, he believes that such a revolt will naturally occur. Upon his own enlightenment, he takes on the responsibility of imparting this newfound knowledge to others:

> Light, of necessity, had to be imparted to the darkened region of the obscure intellects of the slaves, to arouse them from their benighted condition to one of moral responsibility, to make them sensible that liberty was legitimately and essentially theirs, without which there was no distinction between them and the brute. Following as a necessary consequence would be the destruction of oppression and ignorance. (101)

I see Delany's vision of the Black nation as what Benedict Anderson, in *Imagined Communities*, called "the imagined community," in which "in the minds of each [member] lives the image of the communion," (Anderson 6) and the "the nation is always conceived as a deep, horizontal comradeship" (Anderson 7). Blake spends the first half of the novel educating enslaved African Americans in order to develop a mental consensus in the community and a mutual trust. The need for secrecy is necessary due to the lack of trust within the community and the "race traitors" that reveal plots of insurrection to slaveholders in power. The "Black nation" thinking of Delany challenges this loyalty of slaves hoping for approval or inclusion along racial lines; the United States does not include African Americans, leaving them to become a nation within a nation separated by race.

After critiquing the flaws in the family, spirituality, and the quest for inclusion by African Americans in the domestic sphere of North America and after providing a blueprint for change, Delany abandons the possibility for a domestic Black nation. The template that Delany provides consists of the main character understanding the futility of acceptance and inclusion into the nation and then journeying on a quest for a true homeplace. Delany simply separates these through the two parts of the novel and the subsequent authors follow a similar blueprint. That Delany does not completely close the option of a domestic solution, the move to Cuba suggests the importance of other locations.

Although we do not move to Cuba until the second part, Delany's insistence on a Pan-African movement against white supremacy begins with the first chapter. The reader is made privy to the collective efforts of white Northerners and Southerners, Americans and Cubans, to continuing and strengthening the institution of slavery and enhancing the rewards gotten from slavery from being a white man. Through collective actions, regardless of ethnicity or national affiliation, white supremacy reigns supreme. Blake's actions throughout the novel insist that people or African descent must become just as united to fight oppression and white supremacy, as the oppressors are united to strengthen it. Part two of the novel shifts the focus to a global location and examines the ways in which a territory with a Black majority provides a more conducive environment for Black nation-building. The plot moves from North America (the United States and Canada) to Cuba and, briefly, Africa. Cuba is presented as a more viable option for Black nation-building because of its Black (or colored) majority and greater leniency in laws of enslavement and citizenship. Even though the majority of Part Two takes place in Cuba, Africa is presented by Delany as the ultimate territorial homeplace, providing the greatest opportunity for growth (in population, land mass, and economics) and looked upon, by Delany, as the "father-land." The second half of the novel parallels the first half. In comparison to the domestic version of the Black nation, this global version provides greater freedom and empowerment to Black women and the valuing of a spirituality that supports action instead of passivity.

Blake journeys to Cuba partly as a homecoming—this is the place of his birth—but also to find and be reunited with Maggie. Blake reclaims his position as patriarch of his home by removing Maggie from her status as slave. But unlike the illegal means by which he removed his son from the Franks plantation, in Cuba Blake is able to use the law for his purposes. He overhears a conversation among the white planter class that explains the rights of the enslaved:

> This law gives the slave the right, whenever desirous to leave his master, to make him a tender in Spanish coin, which if he don't accept, on proof of the tender the slave may apply to the parish priest or bishop of the district, who has the right immediately to declare such slave free. (183)

Using this right, Blake lawfully restructures his home. He directs Maggie to demand her freedom according to her right and she succeeds. Surprised by her knowledge of the law, her Cuban owner states, "It's all over with her, I see . . . that Cuban Negro [Blake] has taught her this" (185-186). Although Maggie has suffered while in Cuba, her ability to legally reunite with her husband suggests that this global location is more conducive to Black self-determination than North American soil.

The site for the Black nation, as Delany envisions it in its global form, provides the Black man with power unavailable to him in the States, and in following a patriarchal model, Black women play a limited role. But because Maggie has proven herself, the reader is shocked with Blake's new paternalistic treatment of his wife after their union:

> My dear wife, you have much to learn in solving the problem of this great question of the destiny of our race. I'll give you one to work out at your leisure; it is this: Whatever liberty is worth to the white, it is worth to the blacks; therefore, whatever it cost the whites to obtain it, the blacks would be willing and ready to pay, if they desire it. Work this question in political arithmetic at your leisure, wife, and by the time you get through and fully understand the rule, then you will be ready to

discuss the subject further with me. (192)

Such a speech seems unfair as Blake assumes Maggie's lack of knowledge concerning political issues. But Maggie clearly understands the precious value of liberty in ways perhaps Blake cannot; she has paid the price of suffering physical abuse in order to keep her spirit—and her womanhood—intact. Moreover, is not the issue of Black womanhood a political one?

Delany's ambivalence regarding the place of women in the building of the nation is apparent when the major players in the Cuban plan of insurrection are introduced. These are all men, except for their wives, who must be admitted out of obligation but not because they have any voice in nation-formation. While this parallels Delany's own call for the inclusion of women in the process and with voting power at the Emigration Convention of 1858, in the novel the women are presented as less enlightened than the men and are primarily used for introducing questions and issues that need explaining. It is also suggested that the women do not appreciate the gravity of the situation: "The female members of the Council instantly commenced whispering among themselves, all except Abyssa seemingly earnestly engaged" (257). Much in the way Blake had to "awaken" the slaves in the South to their own worth as humans, Delany seems to feel that the women must be enlightened to the necessity for Black self-determination.

The properly redesigned racial home is examined near the end of the novel with the union of Blake and Maggie made legitimate through the marriage ceremony. Once Blake and Maggie are reunited, and his manhood is no longer questioned, he assumes that Maggie must take a background position. But, as he advances, so does she, as Placido explains to her:

> You must remember that there's a great difference between Franks' slaves and General Blake and wife. . . The position of a man carries his wife with him; so when he is degraded, she is also, because she cannot rise

> above his level; but when he is elevated, so is she also;
> hence, the wife of Henry the slave was Maggie the slave;
> but the wife of Mr. Henry Blake will be Mrs. Maggie
> Blake; and the wife of General Blake will be Mrs.
> General Blake. What objections have you to this,
> cousin? (242)

Maggie is taught that her husband's manhood, and his ability to express such, elevates her status just as the attempts to diminish Blake's status through the tarnishing of his wife's womanhood threatened his status.

Just as Maggie's removal at the beginning of the novel marks Blake's awakening, an attack on Black womanhood at the end of the novel is a catalyst for violent response. Abrosina, a colored woman, is horse whipped and stripped of her clothes in the middle of the street as punishment for bumping into a white woman. No one comes to her aid and upon returning to her home, she retorts, "I wish I was a man, I'd lay the city in ashes this night so I would" (313). While the primary responsibility of resisting defilement lies on the Black woman, the Black man is responsible for active protection of the Black home. Abrosina demands action from the Black men of the community:

> One thing I do know, if our men do not decide on
> something in our favor, they will soon be called to look
> on us in a state of concubinage; for such treatment as
> this will force every weakminded woman to place herself
> under the care of those who are able to protect them
> from personal abuse. If they have no men of their
> associations who can, they must find those who will!—
> O, my God, the thought is enough to drive me
> distracted—I'll destroy myself first!" (313)

Such a speech suggests that, without any decision making power in the construction of the nation, women do have some say in the construction of the home. The female characters expect the men of their community to actively participate in the defense of their womanhood, through violent retribution if necessary. Without such action from the men, the women are forced to choose or submit to formations of the home, which do not include Black men. But Delany is clearly not happy with a family and home formation excluding Black men, as can be seen through his presentation of the Draco family.

In Cuba, spirituality is also presented as more conducive to Black political action. Abyssa, in addition to being a Black woman capable of understanding the seriousness of nation formation, is also cognizant of spirituality as action based. The reader's first introduction of Abyssa comes while Blake is on the slave carrier coming from Africa, in hopes of planning a mutiny with the captives on board. Although a captive African, Abyssa is also a converted Christian but not in the tradition of Mammy Judy. Upon recognizing Blake as a "civilized man," she states, "Arm of the Lord, awake!" (224). This introduces the idea that Christianity can be a civilizing tool for those considered heathen but need not be used as a tool for submission and pacification.

As Delany presents it, the forming of a secret organization must include this same form of spirituality that has been so liberating to Blake in the land which he could not consider as homeplace; but it must also be able to justify and support their future plans of necessary violence. Blake explains to his fellow conspirators that, "No religion but that which brings us liberty will we know; no God but He who owns us as his children will we serve" (258). The acts of freedom and liberation become the yardstick by which everything, including spirituality, must be measured; that which does not encourage freedom becomes of no use. In this way Blake and his organizers follow in the path of the oppressors, using only what suits their purposes. While the difference is not stressed, Blake sees himself as seeking a path of uplift for the Black race and not a path of oppression of whites. In response to the question of whether the Black and white races are equal, Blake states, "'Ethiopia shall stretch forth her hands unto

God; Princes shall come out of Egypt'; 'Your God shall be my God, and your people my people,' should comprehend our whole policy" (285).

Once Abyssa is taken into the secret circle of organizers, she often becomes the bridge between the spiritual and the planning of organized violence, important for those who have yet to make that connection. This allows Blake to get to the business of organizing as opposed to having to appease those who see violence as a contrast to their religious beliefs. Abyssa has innate knowledge of what needs to be done regarding the political condition and is comfortable with the idea of necessary violence. Her marriage to Gondolier concretely joins the spiritual and the physical; Abyssa's role is presented as a reminder of the spiritual aspect of Black nation formation, and Gondolier reminds the community that they must not be afraid of using violence to secure their goal.

In *Origin*, Delany asserts a central truth of Freemasonry—"Man the likeness of God"—suggesting three positions of power: Father, Son, and Holy Ghost. He continues, "Man, then, to assimilate God must in his nature, be a trinity of systems—morally, intellectually, and physically" (*Origins* 18). In *Condition*, Delany expands on this idea, taking the theory and making it applicable to life:

> God's means are laws—fixed laws of nature. . . .
> Nothing can be accomplished but through the medium
> of, and conformable to these laws.

> They are three—and like God himself, represented in
> the three persons in the God-head—the Spiritual,
> Moral, and Physical Laws. (*Condition* 38)

When one considers Delany's personal commitment to Freemasonry, in which the realms of the spiritual, moral, and physical are united as a blueprint for proper living, this restructuring becomes a clear extension of his own personal life pursuits; not simply a theory, but a theory that is being put into use.

Delany attempts to apply the Freemasonry theory of moral, spiritual, and physical laws to nation building within his novel through the three male characters of Blake, Placido, and Gondolier. Part one portrays Blake as having no peers in the States. Although Blake is most clearly seen as an embodiment of Delany's Moral Law—"that which is Moral, [can only be accomplished] through the medium of the Moral law. [Men must] exercise their sense and feeling of *right* and *justice*, in order to effect it" (*Condition* 38-39)—Blake must take on moral, spiritual, and physical qualities while in the States.

Placido, introduced in the second half of the novel, while not a man of action, is a priest-poet and spiritual leader. He so perfectly complements Blake as the spiritual guide and spokesman for the movement, that when slave traders intercept a note from Placido to Blake, they assume it is from Blake's wife. Since there is no religious figure involved in the plot and no organized religion to subscribe, Blake having rejected both conjure and the slaveholder's Christianity, it is the poet who gives "the dismissing prayer" in verse at the secret conspiracy meetings. The community of conspirators agree to "know no sects, no denomination, and but one religion for the sake of our redemption from bondage and degradation, a faith in a common Savior as an intercessor for our sins" (258). The power of Placido's poetry, and thus a spirituality which speaks to the people, is described as: "These words, though softly and fearfully spoken were indelibly impressed on every heart, while the sentiments of song, like a lightning flash, ran through every mind" (259). Placido reaches the masses in ways which Blake's logical reasoning cannot. They are stirred into action when they cannot be convinced.

Gondolier represents the physical realm and is presented as admirably militant and shrewd in his anti-authoritarian duplicity. His is the voice that satisfies the need for immediate and direct action. It is important to recognize that the reader is not introduced to Gondolier until well into part two, near the completion of the education and spiritual conversion of the masses. After his own enlightenment, Gondolier boldly asserts to the secret community,

> The instant a person is claimed as a slave, that moment he should strike down the claimant. ...I will resist this night and henceforth every attempt at infringement on my inherent privileges. (255)

Although the reader sees that rebellion is not the first choice of action, and often Gondolier is presented with some humor, he is given the last words of the novel, in response to Ambrosina's public humiliation and speech regarding the need for Black men to act: "Woe be unto those devils of whites, I say!" (313).

It is through the collaborative efforts of these three characters, representing the three natural laws of Freemasonry working together that Delany can imagine a mass unification of people of African descent throughout the Diaspora towards some successful self-determining action which empowers the community separate from white liberal assistance. Delany uses ideas of Freemasonry—a secret and elitist ideology—as a means of educating the masses and resisting racial oppression. Delany's use of mysteries and secrets, both blatant and subtle, played into the very fears of organized Black resistance and mystifies Black identity against which the dominant culture's discourse of power drew its meaning.

The Black nation's development into a major political unit having a territory of great extent under a single sovereign authority is what Scott Nearing, in *The Tragedy of Empire* (1945), describes as coming in stages: the organization of a power nucleus or imperial homeland, the expansion into surrounding alien territory, survival struggle with rival empire builders, and supremacy for the victor.[6] This may also be seen as what Blake explains to his fellow revolutionaries as political economy:

> The foundation of all great nationalities depends as a basis upon three elementary principles: first, territorial

domain; second, population; third, staple commodities as a source of national wealth. The territory must be extensive, population numerous, and the staple such as the world requires and must have; and if the productions be not natural, they must be artificial. (262)

In the novel, Delany examines the issue of population before territory. In the States, Blake develops a community of one political mind—freedom. In Cuba, Blake and his assistants work less on the idea of freedom and more on the idea of blackness as a positive aspect.

Delany's sense of nation presented in the novel is developed from the economic reclaiming of Black labor for one's own use and profit, returning to a previous discussion of the acquisition or stealing of money (that which actually belongs to the slave and is stolen by the slaveholder) by a slave. Blake explains to the members of the secret society that

the African race is now the principle producer of the greater part of the luxuries of enlightened countries ...and that race and country will once again rise to the first magnitude of importance in the estimation of the greatest nations on earth, from their dependence upon them for the great staples from which is derived their national wealth. (261-262)

After restructuring the home and adopting a spirituality that supports action, the Black community is then fully equipped to form a nation capable of becoming a formidable world power. Such success must rely on the community understanding its own talents and energies that have been exploited by white supremacy, and using those same talents and energies toward their own community progress. Blake even suggests that the Black nation, if successful, can reverse the hierarchy of national powers; America, and perhaps Europe as well, can become dependent upon the global Black nation for such crops people of African descent in the Diaspora have experience cultivating—cotton, rice, etc.

Setting the template and issuing the call

Blake, as the first Black nation novel in the African American tradition, poses more questions than it does answers. With his novel divided into two parts, Delany attempts to explore both a possible domestic and a possible global Black nation. This dichotomy divided political strategies of the African American community in antebellum America—the quest for inclusion into the larger nation, or the attempt to emigrate to a foreign land. Delany leaves both options open for further exploration, although he details the global nation section of the novel more thoroughly than he does the domestic nation, which suggests Delany's pessimism about the probability of full inclusion and citizenship in the United States. Leaving both possibilities open-ended, either purposefully or not, renders a call to the next generation of fiction writers and race leaders to more fully explore a solution to white supremacy and the racial exclusion of African Americans from actual citizenship. As a fictional call, *Blake* provides a guide by which to imagine the Black nation in fiction—first to dismantle the quest for inclusion, and then to provide a vision for a Black nation either on domestic soil or in a global version that includes other people of African descent.

Delany's novel introduces questions and ideas that most readers do not associate with early African American fiction: questioning of the productiveness of inclusion, the desire for a separate identity and community, and the connection of African Americans to other people of African descent and other people of color globally. Most important, *Blake* initiates a literary tradition in which the Black nation is imagined and reimagined, according to the changing political status of the African American community.

Double Consciousness and Racial Uplift in Sutton Griggs' *Imperium in Imperio*

It often requires more courage to read some books than it does to fight a battle.

—Sutton E. Griggs.

Martin Delany's *Blake; or, The Huts of America*, the first Black nation novel, provides the template to which subsequent texts in the genre adhered; this chapter seeks to examine how Sutton Griggs imagines the Black nation in fiction by answering Delany's call and revising the template. Delany, writing during the antebellum period, centers nationhood and homeplace on liberation and physical freedom; because Griggs's novel is constructed at the turn of the twentieth century, he, quite naturally, abandons the central importance of freedom in nation building. Moreover, unlike Delany, who explores both a domestic and a global quest for nation building, Griggs places primary emphasis on the prospects for a domestic approach to nation building.[1] This second text in the Black nation novel tradition, *Imperium in Imperio* (1899)[2], appeared only after a forty year gap in the genre; the significance of the break suggests political unrest and a renewed desire for nation building in the Black community. Griggs mounted his critique of how the quest for inclusion into the African American's birthland failed in the Post-Reconstruction era; he offers a comprehensive examination of racial uplift as the means by which African Americans sought full citizenship. Through his depiction of education and patriarchy, responding to the calls of self-determination and locating a real homeplace set by Delany, Griggs generates a scathing commentary on turn of the century social history.

The African American novel published in post-Reconstruction period showed growth and promise, although publication was still on a modest scale. Most of the literature produced at this time generally followed racial uplift ideology, and was assimilationist in nature, although the latter should not always be considered a synonym for the former. The two ideologies, racial uplift and assimilation, have in common the consideration that Black and white Americans are members of the same cultural community. While racial uplift focuses on the outward manifestations of culture (marriage, education, professionalism), assimilation assumes the removal of cultural differences, seen as inferior, and the adopting of dominant society's defining of culturally accepted norms. The racial uplift and assimilationist agendas in most of the literature of this period were exhibited through the protest against the exclusion of African Americans from mainstream American life, specifically middle-class life. Consequently, the literature emphasized ideas of gentility, and promoted a religion of genteel piety. Racial identity was understood to have more to do with a common oppression than a common culture. African American authors at this time attempted to hold to a culture that prized the main features of middle-class American life while living in a society in which the possibilities of entering the American middle-class mainstream appeared increasingly remote. In addition, there was another tension stemming from the unresolved antebellum issue of whether African Americans should stay and make a home in America despite everything, or whether they should emigrate elsewhere.

Imperium is often paired with Delany's *Blake* because of the militant tone and the presentation of a secret political society apparent in both novels. Such a connection leads some literary critics to read *Imperium* as a fictive search for the solution to Black exclusion—separatism and revolutionary violence. Bernard Bell, in *The Afro-American Novel and Its Tradition* (1987), asserts that "*Imperium* vies with *Blake* as the most thematically radical Afro-American novel of the nineteenth century" (61). Bell also states that the novel "announced to the world that blacks would no longer tolerate the denial of their rightful voice in government" (60). In her examination of Griggs as a novelist, Arlene Elder, in *The Hindered Hand*, sees *Imperium* as "a visionary work positing the establishment of a secret, nationwide organization of educated Blacks bent on either a complete redress of grievances or the formation of a separate Black state" (73). Addison Gayle, Jr., in *The Way of the New World*, sees that, in *Imperium*, Griggs "evidences his desire to present a many-sided debate, to focus attention upon the two major ideas in African-American thought and history—nationalism and assimilationism" (73). And lastly, Richard Yarborough, in "The Depiction of Blacks in the Early Afro-American Novel" (1980), concludes that "[i]f Griggs was indeed writing for a predominantly black readership, *Imperium* can be viewed as an attempt, quite likely unconscious, to validate through fictive expression ideas of active black protest and even outright revolt" (490).

Although most critics stress the melodrama in *Imperium*, some literary critics approach the novel through its literary impact. Hugh Gloster, in an early critical examination of the novel, sees *Imperium* as "the first American Negro novel with a strictly political emphasis...[Griggs examined] the passing of the servile black man and hailed the advent of the intellectually emancipated Negro" (13). Wilson Jeremiah Moses, in "Literary Garveyism: The Novels of Reverend Sutton E.

Griggs," credits the novel with being the first "folk novel," and Gayle credits Griggs with being the first to use the term New Negro in a novel. Raymond Hedin, in "Probable Readers, Possible Stories: The Limits of Nineteenth Century Black Narrative," notes that Griggs's narrator in *Imperium*, "Berl Trout, is the first free-standing, first person black narrator in black fiction; he is the first black narrator of an angry work who does not depend for his existence on internal white observers" (198).

Other critics focus on the duality of the African American psyche, defined by W.E.B. Du Bois as double consciousness, and presented in the novel through a double protagonist plot or through the internal war of each protagonist. Wilson Jeremiah Moses, in "Literary Garveyism," sees Bernard as "probably the most striking example of the two souls theme illustrated in an individual character....Also noteworthy, however is Belton Piedmont ...who is torn between his desire to be a loyal patriotic American and his need to fight for racial survival by the use of Un-American tactics" (207). Hedin explains that in the novel, "reason and passion, soul and body, can unite in black men speaking before other blacks" (201).

My reading of the novel is more in line with critics who see Griggs exploring in fiction a critique of African American reliance on education as a strategy for Black success. Dickson Bruce Jr., in *Black American Writing from the Nadir* (1989), asserts that "however political Griggs's works may have been at one level, the novels undercut politics by presenting a bleak, futile vision of American racial life" (157), and also that Griggs "was stressing the desperate condition of black Americans and the lack of clear strategies for change that had a chance of success" (162). Jane Campbell, in *Mythic Black Fiction* (1986), concludes that in *Imperium* "Griggs rejects the myth that education necessarily serves as a tool by which blacks can achieve material success in white society and replaces this notion with an emphasis on education as a process that should develop critical and creative thinking so that blacks can alter oppressive conditions" (50).

Unlike these critics, my examination of *Imperium* sees it as a systematic dismantling of the myth of racial uplift as an effective means towards inclusion. I contend that Griggs does this through the use of a double protagonist plot, not as a means of examining the double consciousness of the African American psyche, but as a presentation of the binary path facing the community relying on racial uplift—inclusion and exclusion. This double protagonist plot responds to the call issued by Delany's *Blake;* although Delany's novel examines divided quests of domestic inclusion or global emigration, Griggs examines a divided quest within domestic inclusion with two protagonists. For Griggs, both sides must come to realize that real inclusion in the American nation is an unrealistic dream when desiring the retention of blackness in the process. If there is a psychoanalytic reading available with this text, I would locate it in Griggs's suggestion that the quest for inclusion by way of racial uplift must be accompanied by a masochistic tendency; racial uplift must include the dismantling of blackness, because blackness is never included, and the quest for inclusion means the consistent rejection of one's blackness. Therefore racial uplift is a limited strategy for Black success in the domestic realm. While *Imperium* extends the Black nation novel tradition by responding to Delany's call for a domestic solution, Griggs does fall into the same limitations as Delany concerning gender politics. Griggs, like Delany, acknowledges and presents the protection of the Black home as a primary catalyst for Black nation building. But because Griggs centers his fictive Black nation on domestic soil, much like Delany does in part one of *Blake*, he is unable to imagine Black women in a leadership role.

The first sign that Griggs is following the dichotomous structure of the Black nation novel is his use of double protagonists, Belton and Bernard. Their most significant similarity is their blackness; the significant difference between these two characters is determined by their connection to dominant society, and thereby, the nation (America). Bernard, by virtue of his mixed heritage and his economic stability, for most of the novel assumes he is included as a part of larger society. Belton, on the other hand, bears the brunt of racism and poverty, and thus becomes the focus for critique in the quest of inclusion by African Americans and racial uplift as the means by which this goal is pursued.

Education in Self-Determination and Domestic Nation Building

Griggs presents the pursuit of racial uplift, by way of education and traditional definitions of manhood, as the means of inclusion into the larger nation. Belton, because of his immediate racial exclusion as a dark skinned Black man, relies more heavily on education for inclusion. Bernard on the other hand, experiencing partial inclusion through some wealth and through his skin color, takes for granted that education will lead to complete inclusion. It is the rejection that each man experiences, despite completing racial uplift and education, which prompts their imagining of a Black nation. Although they originally work towards the same goal, they ultimately have conflicting political ideologies that lead to their separation.

At the beginning of their education, their white male teacher displays obvious bias for Bernard and against Belton, symbolic of the national attitudes for and against the African American community; the dominant society decides which members of the margins, the African American community, are deserving of inclusion. Here, the teacher decides that Bernard deserves inclusion, but not because of anything he has done: "The children all ascribed this partiality to the color of Bernard's skin, and they all, except Belton, began to envy and despise Bernard" (27). Griggs examines how the actions of the dominant society are used to divide the marginalized community. This division, if not repaired, prevents the

55

development of Black autonomy and independence.

The importance of unity as a necessary foundation of the Black nation is clear in *Blake*; Delany, through the main character Blake, addresses the need for unity among Blacks and the necessity of the mulatto class to align with the colored peoples. In *Imperium*, Belton's lack of hatred for Bernard, although Bernard is accepted and chosen for inclusion, is a testament to Belton's understanding of the dominant society's power. Instead, Belton seeks inclusion based on his own merit; the path by which he pursues this quest is through excellence in education, and it becomes the foundation of his competitive drive. Such a response to exclusion—the desire to prove dominant society wrong through excellence—is also examined by W.E.B. Du Bois in *The Souls of Black Folk* (1902), published just after *Imperium*. This desire to prove oneself the equal of dominant society, despite the presence of blackness that is interpreted as inferior, is the foundation for racial uplift.

The choice of graduation speech topics of the two young men show the movement of both Bernard and Belton away from the African American community and instead towards a focus on dominant society. Griggs examines this result as a product of education determined by dominant society and offers this conclusion—the displacement of the racially uplifted from the community—as a critique of racial uplift. Belton's speech, "The Contribution of the Anglo-Saxon to the Cause of Human Liberty," and Bernard's speech, "Robert Emmet,"[3] both present a preoccupation with the dominant society, a valuing of whiteness over blackness. Griggs also presents a foreshadowing of the types of leaders these men will grow into through the choice of speeches. Bernard, choosing to focus on an individual, exhibits a self-centered quality. Although Bernard's choice of Robert Emmet as a subject suggests the identification with a rebellious spirit, we soon see that Bernard is more interested in personal notoriety than community success. His immediate and easy inclusion into dominant society creates a further removal from any concern for the community. Belton on the other hand, choosing to focus on community action (although not his own community), exhibits his inner nature and natural leadership qualities. But because his focus is on the Anglo-Saxon community, we see that he has more of a commitment to dominant society than to the African American community.

Griggs specifically examines education as a foundation for racial uplift through the character of Belton instead of Bernard. Although both men are recruited by Southern schools, which the reader should interpret as "Negro" colleges, Bernard's preference is to go North. Once again, Griggs suggests that inclusion leads the African American away from his/her community. Belton's own pursuit of inclusion, by way of education at Stowe University, is examined as ultimately futile. His interest in attending a Southern school—a Negro college—is significant in two ways. First, it reveals his commitment to the African American community. Second, it further reveals his exclusion from dominant society.

Through Stowe University, we see another instance of Griggs signifying on the limited ability of education (because of its connection to dominant society) to prepare the African American to be fully functioning equal citizens. Just as Harriet Beecher Stowe's presentation of the African American was validated over the portrayal of the community by African American authors, the symbolism of Stowe University suggests the continuation of white authority defining Black needs and desires. Although the University's purpose is Black preparation, it is devoid of Black autonomy. Griggs critiques the effectiveness of education within the system of dominant society to do anything other than continue inequality among the races and Black dependence upon white America; thus, Griggs also questions the usefulness of racial uplift as a strategy for inclusion, since inclusion ultimately signifies the surrender of autonomy. For all of the texts in this study, the critical point for imagining the Black nation (autonomous and separate) appears at the realization of dominant society's ultimate inability to accept blackness, and therefore any inclusion gained remains limited and temporary.

While at Stowe, Belton creates a secret society of students that protest the inferior treatment of the lone Black professor. This strategy is obviously not taught at Belton's school, evident in Belton's acknowledgment of the need for secrecy as well as the teacher's shocked response at the unified front of the students. Moreover, the inclusion of a secret society extends the calls made by Delany and the strategies used by Delany's character, Blake. Griggs continues to present this strategy of secrecy as a vital foundation to nation building by presenting plans as successful. It is a lesson felt by both sides. The young Black students see themselves as change makers and the white authority figures feel the changes made; the former are enthusiastic and the latter are threatened and fearful:

> the confused and bewildered teachers remained behind, busy with their thoughts. They felt like hens who had lost their broods. The cringing, fawning, sniffling, cowardly Negro which slavery left, had disappeared, and a new Negro, self-respecting, fearless, and determined in the assertion of his rights was at hand. (62)

Griggs continues his critique of white involvement in Black education and self-determination. The teachers are not interested in preparing Black liberatory leaders but only in perpetuating a new system of paternalism first fostered by slavery. Griggs thus characterizes education as a preparation for racial equality as hypocrisy without the self-thinking and self-determined Black leadership found in Belton.

Griggs critiques Belton's educational experience as inappropriate for Black leadership partly by noting the passive spirituality upon which it is founded, delivered in the commencement speech of the University president:

"Remember that the kingdom of God is within you. Do not go forth into the world to demand favors of the world, but go forth to give unto the world. Be strong in your own hearts" (65). I have discussed in chapter one with *Blake*, Delany's distrust of Christianity as a useful spirituality for Black liberation due to its promotion of passivity by slave owners, and Delany's quest for a more active spirituality as the foundation for the Black nation. Griggs, a preacher himself, further extends Delany's critique of the Christianity being preached by white authorities to the Black community as a means of pacification, even after emancipation. The president's statement attempts to persuade these "New Negroes," educated and eager to embrace new opportunities of citizenship and inclusion, to be patient with the dominant society ("the world") and to be content with service for the time being. He also suggests: "If you heed my voice you shall become true patriots. If you disregard it, you will become time-serving demagogues" (67). The president assumes that the "New Negro" desires acceptance and inclusion in the nation. But he suggests that path to inclusion is not racial uplift (the education process they have undergone) but passivity. Moreover, he interprets any political action as selfish and fame-seeking. Thus the education process promotes not self-determination and autonomous leadership, but further dependence upon white philanthropy and Black servitude. Belton deeply affected by this speech, and his educational experience in general, takes this advice to heart; his eager adoption of the philosophy, especially when contrasted with his first hand success with changing white supremacist action, initiates the reader's questioning of Belton as a proper race leader. His commitment to the quest of inclusion causes him to blindly follow a path that Griggs believes he should scrutinize more thoroughly.

CHAPTER TWO

Black Women, Manhood, and Domestic Nation Building

With the first part of Belton's racial uplift program completed, he must now pursue the role that will presumably make him acceptable to dominant society; he seeks to prove his manhood through the role of patriarch. Belton attempts this first through marrying Antoinette Nermal; marriage is essential as it is a means of erasing the historical degradation forced on the Black family and the Black woman during slavery. Marriage, in postbellum society, is also viewed as an important marker of humanity and citizenship (along with education and voting—all of which were mandated as illegal for the African American in the antebellum period). Moreover, Belton was schooled in gentility and patriarchy while at Stowe University: "There is hope for that race or nation that respects its women" (82). Griggs presents the union of Belton and Antoinette as suitable due to the equality in their education levels and their commitment to community progress evident in their teaching at a Black school. But Belton's desire to marry comes also with the idea of the male as patriarch and financial provider, and his present position as teacher will not financially support a wife and future children; as a conventional wife, Antoinette must no longer work outside the home. These restrictions, characteristic of racial uplift cause Belton to seek more substantial employment opportunities, commensurate with his education level. Griggs takes this opportunity to examine the reality of opportunities available to educated African Americans, Black men specifically, at the turn of the century.

Belton has been indoctrinated in the belief that education will open doors for him otherwise closed because of racial prejudice. Instead, from his search he finds that education makes Black men and women fairly useless for the job market into which dominant society allows them access. This inability to make proper use of their skills and talents begins Belton's, and those who have been educated

60

like him, questioning of the ideology of democracy upon which the nation is founded: "they [New Negroes] grew to hate a flag that would float in an undisturbed manner over such a condition of affairs" (131). In contrast to the ideas of patriotism Belton is taught at Stowe University, he and other New Negroes begin to see America's hypocrisy as they expect inclusion after education but experience the same exclusion that occurs without education:

> Beginning with passionately hating the flag, they began to think of rebelling against it and would wish for some foreign power to come in and bury it in the dirt. They signified their willingness to participate in such a proceeding. (131)

Griggs extends his examination of American racial exclusion of the New Negro and connects this to Black separatist schemes. Griggs's novel thus continues the dialogue begun by Delany, but also issues a new call: the call to African Americans to align themselves with other people of color ("some foreign power"). This idea is but a seed, though, and Griggs does not allow the planting and harvesting of full separatist thought in this novel. Nor is Belton completely convinced about total racial exclusion.

Committed to financially providing for his family by any means, he submits to dressing in drag to secure employment as a Black woman. His easy ability to secure a position as a domestic, while in drag, initiates for the reader a critique of the connection between economics and racism, as well as dominant society's commitment to dismantling the Black family and Black masculinity. Belton's manhood, as financial provider, is dependent upon the success of his act as a woman. He can only reconcile this dissonance by justifying his cross-dressing as a means of discovering dominant society's attitude regarding African American women. What Belton does discover, the full extent unbeknownst to him previously, is the devaluing of Black female virtue by white men. Griggs's commitment to sexual protection of the African American woman prompts him to refrain from presenting for the reader Black female vulnerability; like all of the male authors in this study, he refuses to risk voyeurism regarding sexual immorality. Instead, by placing the Black male (Blake, Belton, and in chapter three, Bles) in the position of recipient of white lust, these authors are better able to examine and critique sexual immorality as both a threat and a pathology. Moreover, Delany and Griggs present in their novels homoerotic sexual immorality; both Blake and Belton are in danger of being raped by white men. This tactic forces the reader to view the dominant society as a predator on the African American community on many levels.

Belton's understanding of his (and the African American community's) exclusion is complete with the birth of his son. The child is born "white," even though both he and Antoinette are brown-skinned. Belton interprets the birth color of his child as a sign of his failure—failure as financial provider and as recipient of racial uplift. He assumes that Antoinette has submitted to the sexual advances of a white man and given up her virtue: "His feelings toward his wife were more of pity than reproach. Like the multitude, he supposed that his failure to properly support her had tempted her ruin" (137). As husband, he assumes responsibility for her protection as well as her welfare. But the reality of the job market he faced caused him to leave his wife in order to support her, and thus to leave her sexually vulnerable. Dominant society creates obstacles that prevent the African American community from achieving middle class status (racial uplift) and in turn excludes them based on their inability to conform.

The suspected "ruin" of Antoinette forces Belton to recognize the futility in his efforts to assimilate. His inability to create a middle class home prompts him into revolutionary thought:

> Belton had now lost all hope of personal happiness in this life, and as he grew more and more composed he found himself better prepared than ever to give his life

wholly to the righting of his people. (138)

Two important issues are raised from this narrator's statement on Belton's change in political consciousness. First, Belton's original goal of personal happiness consisted of conformity, achieving that which is valuable and a sign of humanity by dominant society: education, financial independence, and a stable family life—middle class respectability. Although he achieves this education, his intelligence is not respected, nor does it provide greater opportunity or break down racial prejudice. Despite his education level, he is forced into manual labor and cannot provide properly for his family. Lastly, he interprets the birth color of his son as his inability to rule his own home. These individual "failures" cause him to abandon a selfish pursuit of progress and focus on the larger exclusion of African Americans from participation in the nation as full citizens. Much in the way that Delany presents Blake's emerging Black nationalist consciousness, Griggs also uses the dismantling of the Black family (Maggie, Blake's wife, being sold in *Blake* and a "white" child being born to Belton and Antoinette in *Imperium*) as the critical sign of exclusion that prompts action.

Second, as was suggested in *Blake*, Belton like Blake, is better able to follow a more militant/revolutionary path without the presence and responsibility of a wife. Participation in the Black family, within a society that devalues blackness, causes desires for conformity and protection of Black womanhood from white male lust. Delany suggests that the Black woman must take this responsibility on herself, committing suicide if necessary, rather than submit to sexual oppression. This in turn would relieve the burden of protection from the Black male and allow him to use his energy for greater political pursuits. Delany also suggests that the foundation of a Black nation must consist of a safe place for Black womanhood, further allowing intellectual progress. Thus Belton's choice to abandon his wife and child and pursue a higher purpose is linked to the need to find safety and protection of Black womanhood. But unlike Blake, who recognizes this safe space as a location of Black majority and Black rule, Belton remains committed to North America, but a transformed North America.

What Griggs explores with the character of Bernard is the undoing of the miseducation given to that section of the African American community that has experienced partial inclusion. Acceptance by dominant society creates a devaluing of African American culture, a trap into which those on the quest for inclusion may easily fall. Bernard's sudden interest in the African American community, for politically ambitious reasons, introduces him to a community he has previously shunned, as we see in his desire to attend Harvard University and his isolation from his classmates as a boy. Unlike Belton who has remained connected to the masses through personal experiences of oppression as well as career choices made, Bernard must first develop a connection to the masses before he can be considered for Black leadership, and he seeks marriage as a means of acceptance into the Black community. As a successful lawyer, he is distant from the community through he experiences, but his attempts to marry Viola are a means of gaining acceptance. Yet, her decision of suicide rather marry one of mixed race, despite her love for Bernard, is reminiscient of Delany's expectations of Black womanhood in *Blake* that Black women should remain pure in the face of white male lust, even if the only alternative is death.

Viola's death propels Bernard into revolutionary action (a pattern of "convenient" female disappearance that we've seen before), yet the difference remains that Viola's absence is final and complete. Viola becomes a greater influence on Bernard's change than Antoinette is on Belton or Maggie is on Blake. Griggs credits the Black woman with the belief in the necessity of separation and the belief that the United States is no homeplace for the African American.

Everything in Griggs's novel prior to Viola's last testament has explored the successes and failures of the quest for inclusion, but neither Belton nor Bernard had given serious thought to separation. Perhaps Griggs feels that Viola can voice this thought because it is the Black woman who is most vulnerable in the quest for inclusion.[4] She presents to him his ability to lead the African American community out of this land of bondage (the United States) and into a land of freedom, a real homeplace.

Secrecy and Domestic Nation Building

It is only after Bernard reexamines the quest for inclusion, following Viola's suicide, that he can be considered for Black leadership and not just personal success. Such an opportunity comes through his alliance with Belton, which Griggs uses once again to contrast his two protagonists. Here the reader is introduced to the title organization, the Imperium in Imperio, secreted in Waco, Texas within the campus of Thomas Jefferson College. The location of the Imperium is significant in two ways. First, the location of Texas, besides being the home state of Griggs, further defines the text as a response to Delany's call. Although in *Blake* Delany suggests that the African American community must abandon any domestic territory as a viable homeplace, in the 1840s Delany himself traveled to Texas to consider it as a possible site for a separate Black state. Thus, Griggs sees Texas as a possible site for a domestic solution. Second, locating the organization within the halls of Thomas Jefferson College signifies a commitment to American democracy in its ideal state.

That Griggs has Belton issue the invitation to membership to Bernard also suggests two things: (1) that such a revolutionary organization/plan must come from the common man, and (2) that although the reader is made privy to the Imperium only in the last third of the novel, its secrecy and connection to Belton suggests its origination with him. The importance of secrecy as a tool in the hands of the disenfranchised is a lesson that Belton learns early and many times over, the most successful example of its use being his coup at Stowe University.

Although the Imperium is a separate organization, its foundation is built upon the African American's exclusion in the American nation: "The Negro finds himself an unprotected foreigner in his own home" (182). Here Belton voices a deep-seated disappointment in American democracy but also a strong connection/patriotism to the nation. This in fact is the continued conflict facing the African American and the issue the community must resolve.

The purpose of the Imperium coincides with the original purpose of racial uplift and thus Griggs attempts to remind his readers of this distinction. The Imperium is

> a society that had a two-fold object. The first object was to endeavor to secure for the free negroes [sic] all the rights and privileges of men according to the teachings of Thomas Jefferson. Its other object was to secure the freedom of the enslaved negroes [sic] the world over. (191)

There is some connection between this organization and Delany's secret society in *Blake* in its hints of freemasonry: "During slavery this organization confined its membership principally to free negroes [sic]" (191).

Bernard, in his presidential message to the Congress of the Imperium, outlines several injustices through which he hopes to persuade the Imperium to action. He first, in addressing the industrial situation, characterizes dominant society's strategy:

> In this great 'battle for bread,' [African Americans] must supply the brute force while [Euro-Americans] will supply the brain. If you attempt to use your brain I will kill you; and before I will stoop so low as to use my own physical power to earn my daily bread, I will kill myself. (211)

Although it is Belton, not Bernard, who has experienced

first hand this response of dominant society to Black intelligence, Bernard sees clearly from the murder of the postmaster the failure of racial uplift to change racist minds. The second point in Bernard's persuasive speech acknowledges the connection of religion and government:

> The Bible which the white people gave us, teaches us that we are men. The declaration of Independence, which we behold them wearing over their hearts, tells us that all men are created equal. ...[But] The monarchial trait seems to not have left their blood. They have apparently chosen our race as an empire, and each Anglo-Saxon regards himself as a petty king, and some gang or community of negroes [sic] as his subjects. (218)

Bernard reiterates here the common understanding that Southern (white) Christianity and American democracy are both hypocritical and co-conspirators in the subjugation of the African American, but he extends this critique to include America's imperialist tendency. To realize how white supremacy is practiced on a global scale is to connect one's fate (success or failure) with other peoples of color in the struggle for independence from white domination. In the conclusion of Bernard's presidential speech, he calls for courage:

> But this much I will say: let not so light , so common, so universal a thing as that which we call death be allowed to frighten you from the path that leads to true liberty and absolute equality. Let that which under any circumstances must come to one and all be no terror to you. (220)

Bernard cannot allow the idea of death be a deterrent because if Viola could give up her life for her beliefs, cannot he do the same and ask that of every man in the Imperium? Moreover his call for courage echoes that of Blake in Delany's novel. Both authors use as a template the rhetoric of America's revolutionary war.

Here, Griggs again connects the quest of inclusion with a tendency toward masochism on the part of African

Americans who retain a hopeful outlook in the face of blatant exclusion. Whereas Bernard's speech illuminates all of the faults and defects in American democracy and therefore the futility in the quest for inclusion, Belton, having never experienced inclusion despite all his attempts at racial uplift, is not ready to abandon hope in a true democracy. Belton begins his argument with, "On her soil I was born; on her bosom I was reared; into her arm I hope to fall in death" (229). Here Belton voices the major obstacle to Black nation formation—the inability to see oneself outside of the birthland. This obstacle also presents itself as the inability to acknowledge a connection to the original birthland—Africa— or to the struggles of other peoples of color. Belton's patriotism to the United States exacts a heavy price in this novel—paid with blood, poverty, rape, and devalued status. Griggs seems to imply that the quest for inclusion in spite of the obstacles (legal, illegal, and immoral) which support exclusion is symptomatic of a masochistic character. Belton's undying pursuit of inclusion, despite his experiences of exclusion, is akin to the abused child that craves love and acceptance from the abusive parent. Dominant society takes on the role of the sadist who must inflict pain on the masochistic Black body.

In order to justify the masochistic tendency to continue his pursuit of inclusion and the hope in a pure democracy, Belton tries to find some reward for the history of African American suffering, symbolic of his Christian, mercenary training at Stowe University:

> Our President alluded to the fact that the negro [sic] was unpaid for all his years of toil. It is true that he was not paid in coin, but he received that from the Anglo-Saxons which far outweighs in value all the gold coin on earth. He received instruction in the arts of civilization, a knowledge of the English language, and a conception of the one true God and his Christ.
>
> While all of the other races of men were behind the ball of progress rolling it up the steep hill of time, the negro [sic] was asleep in the jungles of Africa. (231)

Belton's argument is self-wounding, but indeed an argument taken up by some in the African American community, and certainly by a majority of the dominant society at this time. It is partially a Christian argument, which sees the sufferings of slavery as the means of redemption of the African, and partly an argument based on a very narrow definition of civilization. Belton is quick to accept dominant society's interpretation of Africa as a heathen-jungle land without examination and critique, much in the same way he blindly accepted religious instruction at Stowe University.

Belton's solution to the labor question includes an acceptance of inferior status, if only on a temporary basis:

> The prejudice and pride that prompt them to exclude the Negro from the higher forms of labor, also exclude themselves from the lower forms, thus leaving the Negro in undisputed possession of a whole kingdom of labor. (233)

This argument can be compared easily to Booker T. Washington's argument that fighting for legal rights should be taken up only after first concentrating on financial independence and manual skills. Belton's vision of "a kingdom of labor" is barely one step above slavery, and yet, according to his own argument, the African American has already reaped the rewards of suffering (civilization, English, and Christianity) and should now be released from bondage.

Belton increasingly aligns himself with dominant society rather than his own community when he defines the purpose of racial uplift as creating a more acceptable African American:

> Our grotesque dress, our broken language, our ignorant curiosity, and, on the part of many our boorish manners, would have been nauseating in the extreme to men and women accustomed to refined association. Of course these failings are passing away: but the polished among you have often been made ashamed at the uncouth antics

of some ignorant Negroes, courting the attention of the whites in their presence. Let us see to it, then, that we as a people, not a small minority of us, are prepared to use and not abuse the privileges that must come to us. (235)

Although he came himself from humble and uneducated beginnings, Belton's racial uplift experience has left him unsympathetic to the masses. He now looks upon the folk with a condescending eye, much as the dominant society does. He fails to consider these characteristics which he finds offensive as the natural results of the inferior conditions (poverty, denied education, and lack of opportunities) forced upon the community, and he considers them race specific. He blames the victim and justifies the withholding of natural rights under the law.

Perhaps Belton's most outrageous argument is in defense of mob law:

The shibboleth of the Anglo-Saxon race is the courage of man and the virtue of woman: and when by violence, a member of a despised race assails a defenseless woman; robs her of her virtue, her crown of glory; and sends her back to society broken and crushed in spirit, longing, sighing, praying for the oblivion of the grave, it is not to be wondered at that hell is scoured by the Southern white man in search of plans to vent his rage. (238)

Belton's easy acceptance of protection of white virtue as a justification for lynching once again contradicts his own experiences as a recipient of sexual harassment while cross-dressing and also in believing Antoinette to have conceived a child with a white man. Moreover, his own lynching was justified by the mob by the same faulty argument. What is the reader to make of Belton's arguments which seem so little supportive of Black progress and so easily aligned with the values of the dominant society? I believe Griggs is suggesting that commitment to a domestic solution calls for a certain denial of the level of exclusion faced by the African American. Only in this manner is hope to remain continuous. Along with denial is a commitment to using energy to persuade dominant society to accept blackness as equal, valid, and valuable. Belton concludes his speech with religion and politics:

> We must change the conception which the Anglo-Saxon has formed of our character. We should let him know that patience has a limit; that strength brings confidence; that faith in God will demand the exercise of our own right arm; that hope and despair are each equipped with swords, the latter more dreadful than the former. Before we make a forward move, let us pull the veil from before the eyes of the Anglo-Saxon that he may see the New Negro standing before him humbly, but firmly demanding every right granted him by his maker and wrested from him by man. (244)

Belton's speech, the foundation of which rests on racial uplift, reveals his major concern to be the reception that will be received from the dominant society. Therein, in Griggs's view, lies the fatal flaw with racial uplift, the centering of dominant society in terms of validation, acceptance, persuasion, defining, and power—the unacceptable price of inclusion.

Belton's proposed plan is as follows: (1) reveal to the dominant society the existence of the Imperium as characteristic of the African American love of liberty; (2) convince the dominant society that the African American is ready and willing to live by the doctrine, "Give me liberty or give me death"; (3) spend four years trying to convince the dominant society of existence of the New Negro, but if there is no success, emigrate as a mass to the state of Texas and work within the system with a majority vote; (4) protect by violence the new Black state if necessary; and (5) develop the new Black state apart from the United States (244-245). Belton's plan shows great concern for the larger nation as well as a great hope in the dominant society's change for the better. His continuing hope may be attributed to his experience with benevolent white Americans, particularly with his patron and his professors at Stowe University.

These experiences provide a glimmer of hope among such a hostile reality. Belton's plan also reveals a continued quest for inclusion. Unlike Bernard, Belton's consistent and complete exclusion nurtures a desire for what he has not yet accomplished. Unable to critique the usefulness of inclusion, as Bernard has learned to do, Belton is unable to give up this dream. Thus, although Belton identifies himself and his plan with the New Negro, his beliefs about the African American community and the experience of slavery actually align him with "Old Negro" ideology. Belton's fate represents the dilemma facing the African American community at the turn of the twentieth century, to kill off Old Negro tendencies—not surprisingly, Belton's death in this novel is imminent.

Belton introduces to the Imperium a new tool for revolution; in addition to the sword (war/revolution) and the ballot (transformation through working within the system), he includes the pen. Griggs writes, "If denied the use of the ballot, let us devote our attention to that mightier weapon, the pen" (246). Belton's rejection of the sword is further evidence of his commitment to the idea of inclusion. Griggs has developed for the reader two protagonists who become successful orators, a testament to previous antebellum race leaders such as Douglass and Delany and others who spoke on the abolitionist circuit. The turn of the twentieth century saw an increase in publishing opportunities as well as a confidence in pursuing Black political goals through the written word. Griggs is very self-conscious about the Black author turning to fiction as a means of imagining political theories in action.

Bernard's plan, obviously, is quite different. Although he takes dominant society less into consideration and he dismisses the quest for inclusion, Bernard's motivations as a race leader still are questionable. He foregoes the quest for inclusion in part because, as a Congressman, he feels he has risen as high in dominant society as possible. He also comes to see that inclusion involves limitations and extracts a high price (Viola's suicide). His personal ambition cannot be reached within a system that devalues blackness and therefore his desire lies in creating a system that would foster Black success. He sets out, therefore, to concoct "a scheme that means eternal glory and honor" (250).

Bernard's plan is as follows: (1) keep the Imperium secret from dominant society; (2) purchase the state of Texas and build a military fort with rapid-fire guns secreted in common-place huts; (3) encourage Black men to enter the navy; (4) use the memberships and connections through the navy to develop relationships with the foreign enemies of the United States; (5) hold a Negro fair at Galveston with the Governor, providing an excuse for mass emigration to Texas; (6) seize the capitol during the fair and hoist the Imperium flag; (7) wreck the United Sates navy if need be; (8) demand the surrender of Texas and Louisiana, retaining Texas and using Louisiana as a bargaining chip for acquiring the help of foreign allies. "Thus," Bernard concludes, "will the Negro have an empire of his own, fertile in soil, capable of sustaining a population of 50 million" (252).

Bernard's plan, although it is not blood-thirsty, reveals none of the feelings of patriotism for the dominant national community that are evident in Belton's scheme. Yet Bernard's commitment to a territory on domestic soil reveals little concern for people of color globally nor any sense of self-definition through a diasporic connection to a previous Motherland. Bernard's plan follows an American strategy of imperialism, as well as an American desire for power and empire. Its foundation rests on his conviction that the dominant society will never agree to share its power. As Bernard tells Belton, "I know the Anglo-Saxon race. He will never admit you to equality with him" (253). With Bernard's speech, Griggs summarizes his core critique of racial uplift and the principle of seeking liberation through inclusion. He expresses a strong belief in the totality of dominant society's exclusion of blackness at all costs. Bernard knows that even with money, education, professional success, refinement, and white heritage, he is excluded. He should be a living testament to the success of racial uplift, but instead he is proof of dominant society's commitment to viewing blackness as inferior—his own father would rather commit suicide than face disclosure.

Belton's refusal to adopt Bernard's plan and his resignation from the Imperium turns out to be ruinous. Belton must die, because as he retains traits of the Old Negro mentality, he becomes a danger to the future success of Black autonomy. Griggs suggests, through Belton's obstinacy in refusing to give up his quest for inclusion and his inability to critique dominant society's commitment to devaluing blackness as well as the internalization of dominant society's opinion of the community, that we must kill off that negative influence within ourselves and the Black community before any progress can be achieved. When the Imperium grants Belton thirty days of freedom before carrying out their sentence of execution, this is done to give him an opportunity to see the error of his ways.

Griggs uses the time of the reprieve to wrap up loose ends, namely Belton's marriage and abandoned family. Although the reader probably finds Belton to be a more sympathetic character than Bernard, identifying with Belton's experiences of racism and personal struggle, Griggs reminds us that Belton abandoned his wife without justification and follows a tradition of Black paternal irresponsibility, established by his own father and repeated by him. In reminding the reader of Belton's action, Griggs allows the reader to further critique the suitability of Belton as race leader. His abandonment of Antoinette was based upon his willing acceptance of dominant society's opinion of the Black woman as immoral. Ironically, his efforts to achieve inclusion lead him to the selfish and ignorant act of leaving the Black woman, his wife, and the Black family unprotected. Griggs, like Delany, thus sees the family as the cornerstone of the Black nation. Although Antoinette was a catalyst for stimulating Belton's national work, his vision of the Black nation did not include the Black woman or the family; Belton conveniently forgot Antoinette until his death sentence. But even in realizing his mistaken judgment of Antoinette, he fails to understand one of the most important ingredients for Black nationhood, namely the family unit. Belton justifies to himself foregoing a reunion with Antoinette and their son with his political beliefs. Griggs writes, "He had now learned to put duty to country above everything else" (259). Belton therefore returns to the Imperium to face execution instead of remaining with Antoinette and their son, because he wants to die for his beliefs. Griggs presents Belton's dangerous mentality as one that *must* die, no matter how comfortable the reader and the community is with him. Any ideology that places loyalty to a country hostile to Black humanity and autonomy above the Black family and community must be considered dangerous, diseased, and must be removed.

That Bernard must order the execution is indicative of the change in Black leadership, and the rise of his perspective that the Black nation must begin to think of itself as an imagined community, separate from dominant society, even if remaining on "domestic" soil. For all his determination, though, Bernard does not revel in Belton's execution. "Bernard gazes on Belton with eyes of love and admiration," Griggs writes, continuing, "He loved his friend but he loved his people more. He could not sacrifice his race for his dearest friend. Viola had taught him that lesson" (260-1). Bernard's sympathy for Belton is symbolic of the New Negro's acknowledgement of the Old Negro's coping strategies. While these strategies were appropriate for a previous era, Bernard sees them as obsolete in the present moment of the novel. Just as the position of the African American has changed, from legal enslavement to official freedom, so too must the strategy of the community change. Belton must change his viewpoint away from seeking inclusion into dominant society, a lesson he failed to learn through his own struggles and his marriage.

Belton's dying words reflect an interpretation of Du Bois's double consciousness. In his final speech, Belton proclaims,

> Tell posterity...that I loved the race to which I belonged and the flag that floated over me; and being unable to see these objects of my love engage in mortal combat, I went to my God, and now look down upon both from my home in the skies to bless them with my spirit. (261)

The inner conflict that Du Bois presents as within the African American is externalized in Belton's fear of an outer conflict between his race and "the flag that floated over me." Belton does not suffer an inner conflict because his double consciousness is not developed; despite his experiences with racism, Belton is able to see himself as dominant society does, but unable to view dominant society with the critical edge of second sight. Moreover, he also has a reliance on God, a passive nature, and an acceptance of the promise of heavenly rather than earthly reward, all of which are traits or perspectives typically linked to Old Negro political orientation. The Imperium buries Belton with the American flag, symbolizing the death of the Old Negro along with the desire for inclusion into the nation.

Griggs ends *Imperium* much in the way Delany ends *Blake*—with no complete imagining of a revolution that breaks from American dominant society. He continues Delany's interest in secrecy as the only viable means of progress within white supremacy. He also continues to examine the vulnerable state of Black womanhood as a catalyst for Black male militancy and nation building as the work and responsibility of Black men. Griggs differs from Delany in several ways, including their critiques of Christianity and their imagining of the role of women in the nation building process. Although Griggs presents problems with the Christianity espoused by Belton, he does not advocate a new form of spirituality as a foundation or unifying feature of the Black nation. And whereas Delany imagines women playing a marginal role in nation building, he at least includes women in his discussion of it. Griggs, on the other hand, is unable to imagine women taking any role except homemaker, while Black men attempt on their own to solve the problem of exclusion.

CHAPTER THREE

Pauline E. Hopkins Calls for Gender Inclusion in *Of One Blood*

No people are ever elevated above the condition of their females; hence the condition of the mother determines the condition of the child.

—Martin R. Delany

The colored woman of to-day occupies, one may say, a unique position in this country. In a period itself transitional and unsettled, her status seems one of the least ascertainable and definitive of all the forces which make for our civilization. She is confronted by both a woman question and a race problem, and is as yet an unknown or unacknowledged factor in both.

—Anna Julia Cooper

As the African American community debated the possibility of inclusion and acceptance in the United States in the face of blatant exclusion, the post-Reconstruction period also witnessed a revival of the idea to develop some outside territory with a Black majority as the necessary foundation for African American success. The Black nation novel, in its post-Reconstruction manifestation, reemerged with two variations that build upon the domestic/global dichotomy identified previously as a structuring device in

Martin Delany's *Blake*. The domestic Black nation narrative, illustrated in Sutton Griggs's *Imperium in Imperio*, attempts to imagine a Black community as racially separate and yet an integrated part of the United States. In contrast, the global Black nation narrative assumes a territory based outside of North American soil and inclusive of all peoples of African descent within the Diaspora. Though typically marginalized and dismissed in existing literary historical accounts, Black nation novels from the post-Reconstruction period should be seen as an important part of the general exploration of separatist possibilities that characterize this moment in African American social history.

Although published during the same era as Griggs, Pauline Hopkins's last novel, *Of One Blood* (1902)[1], reveals less optimism than other contemporary novels about the transformation of the United States into a more livable homeplace for African Americans. Hopkins provides a counter narrative to Griggs's imagined domestic Black nation. Following the template set by Delany, Hopkins begins with an examination of the futility of a domestic Black nation and then shifts her focus to a global homeplace—Ethiopia.[2] Similar to Griggs, she critiques both racial uplift as the means by which African Americans sought full citizenship and how the quest for inclusion failed in post-Reconstruction America. Hopkins breaks from Griggs by evaluating the desire to pass for white as racial uplift gone awry; she recognizes, far better than Griggs, the dominant society's legal and violent commitment to racial exclusion at the turn of the twentieth century. She continues to examine the issue, begun by Delany, as to the importance and position of Black women in nation building strategies, especially as it pertains to the construction of the Black family. This chapter examines how Hopkins imagines the Black nation in fiction, placing primary emphasis on the necessity for a return to an African homeplace, if not physically then spiritually, and placing greater emphasis on the Black woman's inclusion.

Until recently, Pauline Hopkins was overshadowed by Frances Harper's success, but like Delany and Griggs, her contributions have been recently resurrected. Hopkins was virtually forgotten until Ann Allen Shockley rediscovered her work in 1972.[3] Since then her reputation has gradually reemerged.[4] In *Reconstructing Womanhood: The Emergence of the Afro-American Women Novelist* (1987), Hazel V. Carby presents Hopkins and Harper as equal contributors to the rejection of true womanhood as an exclusive white only ideology, claiming and creating of a space for Black women within sentimental fiction. The collection of critical essays, *The Unruly Voice: Rediscovering Pauline Elizabeth Hopkins* (1996), begins a greater in depth examination of Hopkins as a major literary figure of the turn of the twentieth century. All of Hopkins's works have been reprinted, along with those of many other of her contemporaries, as numerous forgotten nineteenth-century feminist and Black nationalist texts are being recovered and given new consideration.[5]

In 1900, Hopkins began a career as editor of, and frequent contributor to, the newly founded *Colored American Magazine*, a Boston African American literary journal. In "The Story of Our Magazine," R.S. Eliott, another *CAM* editor, wrote of Hopkins the following:

> Her ambition is to become a writer of fiction, in which the wrongs of her race shall be handled as to enlist the sympathy of all classes of citizens, in this way reaching those who never read history or biography. (47)

Hopkins saw her editorial position as useful for social, political, and creative discussions pertinent to the African American community. Her own publications in the journal show her commitment to literature as a pedagogical source for historical information, and *CAM* became a teaching tool for African American readers, an agent of social intervention, and an important showcase of editorials and imaginative literature.[6] Hopkins, in her contributions, consistently shows a commitment to racial uplift theories as well as a desire to broaden the reading public's awareness of contemporary social issues and of African American history outside of the United States. Her most detailed attempts at racial uplift, and in her last novel her critique of racial uplift as a viable strategy for racial inclusion, echo the concerns of Griggs discussed in the previous chapter.

Hopkins's literary contributions include two dramas, eight short stories, four novels, one full length study on race, and numerous articles and biographies.[7] In her earlier works, she envisioned worlds more humane than that of turn-of-the-century America and developed a template for race relations that was, in many ways, far ahead of its time. In her last novel, *Of One Blood* (1902), her revised view of the world, choice of an ancient African setting, and the novel's rather ambiguous ending indicate that, by the end of her literary career, Hopkins was beginning to see problems in the wholehearted assimilationism of her earlier works. Both Ethiopianism and a civilizing mission are central determining ideas in this text. In its evocation of ancient Africa, *Of One Blood* and her study on race, *A Primer of Facts Pertaining to the Early Greatness of the African Race and the Possibility of Restoration by Its Descendants* (1905), show a writer moving toward an affirmation of Black distinctiveness.

Hopkins's first three novels follow the sentimental novel tradition, while *Of One Blood* breaks this pattern by centering on national and international rather than exclusively domestic scenes, through the story of three siblings—Reuel, Dianthe, and Aubrey. I believe that her earlier texts are attempts to promote the possibility of a Black nation *within* the United States through racial uplift ideology. Her last novel, though, suggests that she has recognized the futility of efforts to build a Black nation domestically and the dangers of assimilation as a foundation for African American success. Although Reuel is in the end a success story in *Of One Blood*, he is unable to protect his sister, Dianthe, or his brother, Aubrey, from the corruption of a racist society. His own mistreatment of

Dianthe, denying her blackness and leaving her unprotected and in the hands of a "white" man in order to pursue material wealth, shows the destructive influence of racist America on him. His personal success comes only after he experiences the counter-influence of a positive African community. Instead, *Of One Blood* promotes a global Black nation through the acceptance of a rich and positive African heritage. In this novel, then, Hopkins can be seen as adopting the bifurcated plot line template established by Delany in *Blake*. But while her characters do physically travel to Africa, and thus reprise some of the emigrationist ideas expressed by Delany, Hopkins seems more committed to the idea that African American success is dependent upon an emigration of the mind, not necessarily of the body.

Of One Blood, like Delany's *Blake*, is a blend of genres—gothic novel, science fiction, romance, detective fiction, and passing novel—and is sometimes viewed as incoherent. Because of the novel's "near-white" passing characters and the opening scene, literary critics rely on and usually limit interpretation to a psychoanalytic reading, focusing on the desire to pass for white, the mental despair caused by passing, and the melancholy associated with racial limitations. Cynthia D. Schrager, in "Pauline Hopkins and William James: The New Psychology and the Politics of Race," asserts that "the novel both exploits the new psychology about the indeterminacy of racial subjectivity and figures racial identity in terms of a more deterministic discourse of blood" (Schrager 184). In "Hysteria and Trauma in Pauline Hopkins's *Of One Blood; Or, the Hidden Self*," Deborah Horvitz asserts that "as an 'hysteric,' Dianthe represents—or, more precisely, her body represents—the site of convergence of violence, racism, and misogyny" (245).

Elizabeth Ammons, in *Conflicting Stories* (1992), takes a unique viewpoint choosing to focus on Dianthe as an artist (Fisk Jubilee Singer) and "the tremendous power that in Hopkins's view is contained in the Black woman artist: her spirituality, erotic energy, and indestructibleness" (82). Ammons gives the character of Dianthe more consideration than most critics as a pawn in the struggle for power between Reuel and Aubrey. Following in that line of examination, Jacqueline K. Bryant, in *The Foremother in Early Black Women's Literature* (1999), focuses on Aunt Hannah and Mira as mother figures who impart truth to Reuel and Dianthe and pass on the royal legacy.

Although *Of One Blood* is the first text in this study that presents a fully functioning "homeplace" outside the United States and a story of emigration to such a place, most literary critics do not interpret the end of the novel, the return to Telassar by Reuel and Aunt Hannah, as connoting advocacy of emigration. Hazel Carby simply takes "the discovery of Reuel's heritage [to be] the discovery of Pan-Africanism" (*Reconstructing* 158). Thomas J. Otten, in "Pauline Hopkins and the Hidden Self of Race," claims that "[e]xcavating the depths of black character...yields a Pan-African understanding of racial history" (230). Other literary critics see *Of One Blood* as an extension of Hopkins's examination of racial uplift in her previous works. Jeannie Kassanoff, in "'Fate Has Linked Us Together': Blood, Gender, and the Politics of Representation in Pauline Hopkins's *Of One Blood*," sees "the interconnected corporeal issues of blood and gender that inform Hopkins's novel effectively deconstruct[ing] the monolith of the New Negro by questioning its contours and its limitations" (160). And Kevin Gaines, in "Black Americans' Racial Uplift Ideology as 'Civilizing Mission'," asserts that "[t]he Pan-African vision of *Of One Blood* linked domestic uplift ideology to the idea of the civilizing mission, but in a nostalgic manner that imagined black Americans' reclamation of an ancient African civilization as a refuge from contemporary domestic and imperial oppression of colored peoples" (445).

Finally, some literary critics see the underground nation of Telassar as compensatory fantasy. As John Gruesser claims in "Pauline Hopkins's *Of One Blood*:

Creating an Afrocentric Fantasy for a Black Middle Class Audience," Telassar is simply "a fantasy that restores to Africa its former greatness but also a more local and much needed fantasy, one in which a white American character must answer for racial prejudice and legal segregation" (16). Gaines suggests that those writers struggling with racial uplift ideology, and "laboring under ethnocentric dismissals of Africa ...intensified their desire for a true homeland, even one of the imagination" (Gaines 434).

Ethiopianism was as literary as it was political and religious. In 1829, Robert Alexander Young published *The Ethiopian Manifesto, Issued in defense of the Black Man's Rights in the Scale of Universal Freedom*. In it he predicted the coming of a messiah who would "call together black people as a nation in themselves" (8). In the same year, David Walker published *An Appeal in Four Articles; Together with a Preamble, to the Coloured Citizens of the World* in which he conveyed a spirit of apocalyptic Christianity.[8] Henry Highland Garnet, in *The Past and Present Condition, and the Destiny of the Colored Race* (1848), provided Africa with a glorious past, describing the achievements of ancient Egypt and Ethiopia, and quoted Psalm 68:31 as a sign of greater things to come. And Delany, in *Condition*, emphasized the special mission of African American emigrants in the regeneration process of Africa. Ethiopianist thought reached a new level of complexity in the nineteenth century through the writings, sermons and activism of Alexander Crummell, who stressed the religious and spiritual aspects of African redemption, and Edward Blyden, who paid more attention to the political and economic prerequisites for Black self determination.[9]

My examination of Hopkins's *Of One Blood* takes a different focus than most critics, although I find the feminist readings of Hopkins's text very valid. While it is clear that Hopkins examines the ways in which race is a limiting social construction, I disagree with interpretations that suggest that she uses passing characters as an indication that the markers of race we use are invalid. African American fiction writers have used the passing novel to explore and protest the color line, but more often than not passing characters eventually reject whiteness, and the authors promote race loyalty and solidarity. The decision to pass is usually brought about by a desire to escape slavery and/or oppression, avoid racism, and/or improve financial status. African Americans unable to pass for white attempted to overcome these obstacles through strategies of racial uplift, which include education, moral reform, sound family life, and professionalization. Successful passing characters are successful because they have already acquired the outward manifestations of racial uplift, allowing easy blending into dominant society. Hopkins uses the genre of the passing novel to explore and critique the ways in which racial uplift as a strategy for inclusion falls short. Therefore, I believe that most psychoanalytic readings—of Reuel's depression, Dianthe's hysteria and amnesia, and Aubrey's homicidal tendencies—are detached from the cultural context of complete racial exclusion in America and therefore lose their persuasive force.

Moreover, my examination of this Hopkins text, when the proper cultural backdrop is established—Ethiopianism, civilizationism, and the quest for inclusion and homeplace— shows the author reevaluating previous assertions that the United States is a possible home for African Americans. In the Black nation novel tradition, Hopkins clearly offers a response to Delany's call for a global Black nation. She also thinks further than Delany about the usefulness of Christianity as a spirituality for the Black community, the role of Black women in nation formation, and the necessity for establishing and protecting the proper racial home as a foundation for the Black nation. Where her contemporary Griggs, remains focused on domestic freedom struggles, Hopkins opens a window into the global concerns of dispersed Africans at the turn of the twentieth century.

The Black Woman as the Foundation of the Nation

The formation of the Black nation in *Of One Blood* begins by critiquing the quest for inclusion in the domestic nation: it emphasizes the difficulty in America for African Americans to structure safe and productive racial homes. Anna Julia Haywood Cooper, in "Womanhood A Vital Element in the Regeneration and Progress of a Race," wrote in 1886, "A stream cannot rise higher than its source. The atmosphere of homes is no rarer and purer and sweeter than are the mothers in those homes. A race is but a sum of all its parts, so the character of the parts will determine the characteristics of the whole" (Cooper 64). While *Of One Blood* departs from the sentimental novel, Hopkins still presents the virtuous Black female as the determinant of African American success. The Black nation novel, in its domestic version, offers a collective attempt to imagine strategies of Black family empowerment and community success; but here Hopkins critiques the idea that racial uplift is an effective means towards this end. Hopkins suggests that racial uplift is an extension of the plantation system that places the Black woman in a vulnerable state, unprotected from white male lust, and thereby leaves the foundation of the family—and, following Cooper, we could add, the nation—insecure and unstable.

In the novel, Aubrey Livingston has succeeded in ultimate inclusion—he is assumed by all to be a white man. Although he had no hand in his coup and does not even know of his own success, the reader sees that his inclusion is so complete that he participates in the exclusion of others, specifically Reuel and Dianthe. Although the three are siblings, Reuel is handicapped in a way that Aubrey is not—Reuel knows of his own blackness. Because he risks being discovered, he feels compelled to hide all traces of blackness (even "Black thought") and he suffers emotional turmoil from this tension. Reuel's inclusion can never be as complete as Aubrey's, so Reuel does the next best thing—he passes for white.

At the beginning of the novel, Reuel suffers from melancholy, which the reader associates with his "hidden self" (also the subtitle of the novel), the denying of his racial identity in an effort to reach professional success. Although he has attempted to fully assimilate into American culture—defined here as white culture—Hopkins emphasizes his inability to dismiss and devalue all blackness. Although his fellow classmates suspect that he is not white, they accept his otherness because they do not suspect his blackness; Reuel is seen as different, but not as Black. Yet, Reuel cannot enjoy his success because he always risks discovery, and he is not willing to fully give up that which is necessary for full inclusion—blackness. In his melancholy state, Reuel envisions a woman, "a fair face framed in golden hair, with soft brown eyes, deep and earnest—terribly earnest they seemed just then—rose-tinted baby lips, and an expression of wistful entreaty" (445). Uncomfortable with this power of mysticism that he has, Reuel dismisses the visions as "the effect of the imagination" (445). But the fading of this female image leaves Reuel with "a sense of sadness and foreboding" (445), suggesting that what he longs for and needs can be obtained through this woman. His vision soon takes concrete form as Dianthe Lusk, when Reuel attends a concert of the Fisk Jubilee Singers: "there before him in the blaze of light—like a lovely phantom—stood a woman wearing the face of his vision of the afternoon" (454). Reuel's refusal to completely assimilate is shown through his open attraction to Dianthe, the Black woman.

Dianthe, although able to cross the color line due to her fair skin, willingly claims blackness as a member of the Fisk Jubilee Singers, and yet she is also presented as a tortured soul. After the concert, Dianthe comes to Reuel a second time, physically but still mysteriously, along a path of hemlock trees, in a state of grief. She says to him, "You can help me, but not now; tomorrow. ...The time is not yet" (461-2). Coincidentally, the next day Reuel gives her medical attention after she is hurt in a train accident, remembering her request for help the day before. Although Dianthe is "cold and stiff" with death (463), Reuel possesses the skills to revive her: "Advancing far afield in the mysterious regions of science, he had stumbled upon the solution of one of life's problems: *the reanimation of the body after seeming death*" (464). Reuel successfully resuscitates Dianthe from her "suspended animation" (465), and explains to the other doctors that, "The secret of life lies in what we call volatile magnetism—it exists in the free atmosphere" (468). Here Reuel is speaking specifically of physical life in contrast to death; but his statement can also be interpreted as Hopkins's examination of the pursuit of life, liberty and citizenship by African Americans. The volatile magnetism can be seen as the quest for inclusion into a nation committed to the exclusion of blackness. This attraction to a birthplace one cannot call home is metaphorically magnetic. The attraction is also usually volatile, in the sense of explosive, as seen through the legal and illegal racial violence committed against the African American community, but it is also volatile in the sense of fleeting: the constant changing of the "rules" makes inclusion an ever-elusive goal. Such volatile magnetism, in fact, encompasses death, if not physical, then emotional, such as Reuel's depression and Dianthe's amnesia. The free atmosphere which holds the secret of life, although technically floating above the gravitational pull of the earth's surface, for the purposes of this reading, is that homeplace in which one is truly free to express all parts of him or herself, including and especially one's blackness. In this novel this free atmosphere cannot be located in the U.S. where inclusion is only granted by whites and blackness is wholly erased.

In an attempt to "uplift" Dianthe, Reuel uses her amnesia as an opportunity to transform her into a "white" woman, the "help" he assumes she needs and wants. Although Reuel is suffering because he denies his own blackness and passes, he assumes this "transformation" of

Dianthe will not cause her to suffer, due to her lack of knowledge about her blackness. He also assumes that marriage to him, as a "white" man, will give her the protection she may be seeking in society. Moreover, although Dianthe has sought out Reuel in visions, he does not assume that she seeks a connection with blackness; rather, he assumes that she seeks inclusion as he does.

Hopkins presents Dianthe as also having mesmeric powers and talents. Yet even in her amnesic state, she remains more connected to blackness than Reuel. While still in the hospital, she tells him, "I see much clearly, much dimly, of the powers and influence behind the Veil, and yet I cannot name them. Some time the full power will be mine; and mine shall be thine" (475). Hopkins uses the term "Veil", a signifier of race and exclusion, to suggest that Dianthe acknowledges power in racial acceptance, identification, and separateness. In *The Souls of Black Folk* (1903), W.E.B. Du Bois explains that "the Negro is a sort of seventh son, born with a veil, and gifted with second-sight in this American world,—a world which yields him no true self-consciousness, but only lets him see himself through the revelation of the other world" (38). This realization is a dull memory for Dianthe while she is in the hospital, because she does not really *know* who she is. Her ignorance of her personal history can be interpreted as Reuel keeping her identity from her, or, in a larger sense, her lack of knowledge that blackness includes greatness prior to enslavement on North American soil. Either way, Hopkins connects knowledge with the acquisition of voice when Dianthe states, "and yet I cannot name them [the powers and influence behind the Veil]." Without the necessary historical knowledge, Dianthe is unable to access the power she vaguely knows exists within blackness, "behind the Veil." Moreover, Dianthe expects that her acquisition of this vaguely felt power will benefit her community (Reuel) instead of a being just a personal victory ("and mine shall be thine").

Because Dianthe is kept away from the truth she craves, she is forced to rely on Reuel's strategies for success, which include passing, a symptom of the quest for inclusion when faith in racial uplift no longer exists. Hopkins's characters, in the terms of double consciousness set forth by Du Bois, are unable to be Americans and Negroes without the images of the latter producing strong emotional turmoil. Thus in order to be productive Americans, they feel they must pass; in Dianthe's case, Reuel believes she must pass as well, although unwillingly and unknowingly. As I have explored previously, with Delany's *Blake* and Griggs's *Imperium in Imperio*, the direction for the Black nation (domestic or global) suggested by the author of each of these novels correlates with the direction of the characters' responses to exclusion and inclusion. If the character's desired goal is inclusion into the American nation, we must examine who is included and why, as well as who is excluded and what they do about it. Hopkins here examines and critiques attempts at inclusion that are accompanied by desires to minimize, "transcend", or otherwise erase "blackness" as much as possible. One such attempt includes trusting and valuing whiteness over blackness, as Reuel mistakenly trusts Aubrey and decides to divulge Dianthe's secret blackness to him but not to her. Reuel confides in Aubrey his plans to marry Dianthe and to never tell her that she is Black. Believing that he himself is successfully passing, Reuel justifies this plan by explaining, "There is no sin in taking her out of the sphere where she was born" (479). Thus Reuel uses his transformation of Dianthe into a "white" woman and the wife of a "white" doctor as an extreme but self-negating form of racial uplift.

Aubrey's reaction to this news reveals Reuel's own ignorance of dominant society and his false sense of inclusion. Reuel proves to be a bad judge of character; with his knowledge of their racial identities, Aubrey holds tremendous power over both Reuel and Dianthe. Passing in order to be included, unlike racial uplift, always carries with it the threat of exclusion by way of racial discovery. Thus Aubrey holds the trump card of exclusion through his knowledge of Reuel's and Dianthe's blackness. Understanding that he knows of Reuel's blackness, Aubrey forces Reuel to vocalize an opinion on the race question: Reuel finally admits, "I have a horror of discussing the woes of unfortunates, tramps, stray dogs and cats and Negroes— probably because I am an unfortunate myself" (449). He attempts to take on the dominant view by placing African Americans in the same category as tramps and animals, giving the community (and himself) subhuman status, ignoring the transforming power of racial uplift, and labeling himself as an unfortunate. Yet another part of him desires connection with that which he is denying publicly. His statement is almost a confession of his deception; while this may be connected to his state of financial insecurity, it can also be interpreted as a confession of blackness created out of the emotional turmoil of passing. Yet in this scene, Hopkins effectively relates the sadomasochistic relationship between the African American desirous of inclusion and the nation that blatantly excludes all forms of blackness while creating false hopes of possible inclusion.

Reuel's intense feelings are borne from his knowledge that Dianthe is a Black woman, and what he believes is his success in helping and protecting her. She, in contrast, cannot love him wholeheartedly because she does not know herself, nor does she know the true Reuel, the Black Reuel. What she does realize is that she is missing some knowledge that she assumes to be empowering. And yet she feels some connection to Reuel through their shared experience with mysticism. Despite her lack of romantic love for him, she agrees to marry him, perhaps because he seems so sure about the path through life.

In contrast to her cold affection for Reuel, Dianthe is noticeably repulsed by Aubrey: "she shudders everytime he draws near, and sinks to the ground under the steady gaze of his eye" (501). Unlike Reuel, who projects vulnerability from living a life of deceit and labels himself an unfortunate, Aubrey operates from a sense of entitlement. Although Dianthe does not understand why, she senses that Aubrey is a danger to her. The danger stems from the history of white male oppression of Black womanhood, but she does not realize it; nor does she act on this sensation because she has come to trust in Reuel's judgment. The reader sees, however, that Reuel is a poor judge of character, his skill having been corrupted through his quest for inclusion. How can he judge properly when seeking acceptance from a society committed to rejecting every part of him? Reuel trusts Aubrey as a confidante and advisor, but is unable to see that Aubrey does not act in his best interest. Reuel's quest for inclusion causes him to value the very people that are most committed to excluding him because they are the people able to grant inclusion.

When Dianthe eventually accepts his marriage proposal, Reuel becomes anxious about his ability to find employment and seeks out Aubrey for advice. Aubrey's primary concern is separating Reuel and Dianthe, and the reader suspects that he has had some hand in Reuel's unemployment. Knowing Reuel's desire for inclusion, Aubrey baits him with the markers of membership in society—money and glory. But concurrently, Aubrey implicitly reminds Reuel that he will never reach full inclusion by connecting the expedition to the good of the Negro race. Reuel must now decide which he values more: a life with Dianthe or professional success. His choice symbolizes the dilemma of the African American pursuing inclusion. Either Reuel values personal acceptance and validation of all parts of himself, even his blackness, as he hopes that Dianthe will eventually regain her memory; or he values materialism which can only be gained through a rejection of his connection to blackness. As we have seen previously, Reuel attempts a compromise; he marries Dianthe, but immediately joins the expedition to Ethiopia which Aubrey has set for him, thus leaving the Black woman in Aubrey's care.

Prior to departure, Dianthe once again appeals to Reuel for the knowledge she needs:

> Do you know, I sometimes dream or have waking visions of a past time in my life? But when I try to grasp the fleeting memories they leave me groping in darkness. Can't you help me, Reuel? (499)

The assistance Dianthe desires from Reuel is a reconnection with her blackness. But he cannot provide this kind of assistance because he himself is disconnected. Instead, he attempts to persuade her to forget her past (her blackness and her previous exclusion) and to enjoy her new and present life. But in recalling Dianthe's statement in the hospital—"Some time the full power will be mine; and mine shall be thine" (475)—the knowledge she seeks brings power, not only for herself but for him as well. Reuel, in pursuit of material wealth, leaves Dianthe with Aubrey but without knowledge of herself. He thus disempowers Dianthe by not telling her the truth, while at the same time empowering Aubrey with the knowledge of her racial identity.

Whereas Reuel attempted to "save" Dianthe by denying her blackness, Aubrey's strategy is to reveal to Dianthe that her blackness is a liability that he alone is willing to subsume. Reuel's "desertion," his pursuit of material success, allows Aubrey to define blackness negatively, in hopes of making Dianthe indebted to him; but Dianthe remains repulsed by Aubrey and attempts to resist him. He cannot have Dianthe as a "white" woman because she is married to Reuel. He believes, though, that he can obtain her as a Black woman, falsely negating her marriage to Reuel and creating a dependency on him for inclusion and acceptance. He removes the Black male from her life in order to blackmail her into submission. Even with all this persuasion, Dianthe does not submit willingly and therefore Aubrey decides to take her by force. Aubrey keeps Dianthe sequestered until he tells her Reuel is dead; she submits to marry him in a state of grief and is then hidden away on his family plantation. Although they are now "married," Dianthe never grows to love Aubrey.

Aubrey, a "Black" man fully included in American society and therefore in society's eyes a "white" man, takes on the role of plantation owner in two ways. First he removes the "Black" man (Reuel) from the racial home by sending him off on an expedition, a quest for money and glory he is unable to acquire in the States. Second, he appropriates the "Black" man's wife for his own and rapes her. It is important to note that Aubrey takes Dianthe to his family plantation where he coerces and blackmails her into a sexual liaison. The tyranny Dianthe suffers under Aubrey's hands represents historical plantation exploitation and post-Reconstruction Jim Crow exploitation and abuse. However, the tyranny Reuel has inflicted on Dianthe, although Hopkins presents it as life giving and genuinely loving, also represents historical plantation exploitation, but in a different way: Reuel reenacts dominant society's practices of keeping the enslaved community ignorant and censored. Dianthe is ignorant of her own racial history, and the African American community, Reuel included, is ignorant of its own history prior to North American enslavement. Dianthe contributes to her own censoring because she is taught by Reuel to suppress her faint memory of a past as a means of obtaining acceptance. As her racial memory returns, while she is in Aubrey's keeping, she is too ashamed of her blackness, caused by valuing dominant society's definition of blackness, to tell her husband for fear of rejection and exclusion. The African American community self-censors because exposure of blackness threatens possibilities of inclusion.

Elizabeth Ammons notes that the plantation system mentality, as inscribed by Hopkins in the novel, divides Black men and women, removing and thus disempowering the former and appropriating and controlling the latter through rape. But I believe that what Hopkins is exploring more broadly is how that system of accommodation and assimilation, as well as the plantation system, disempowers the Black family and thereby the possibility of a domestic Black nation. While it is obvious that Hopkins exposes the white patriarchal plantation owner, as cruel, amoral, and disruptive of the Black family pre-emancipation, she also critiques potentially self-destructive values found in the Black community, post-Emancipation. Reuel, in colluding with Aubrey by assigning Dianthe a fictitious white identity, directly enables Aubrey to exploit and blackmail her. Moreover, such analysis takes on the status of self-critique on Hopkins's part since the preferences for inclusion and assimilation that Reuel and Dianthe exhibit are preferences that Hopkins has supported in her own previous novels.

Dianthe also exhibits periods of empowerment associated with her alignment with blackness. First, before her amnesia, Dianthe fully claims blackness, despite her ability to pass for white, through her association with the Fisk Jubilee Singers. This association also suggests her dedication to promoting value in blackness as the group tours and performs what is specifically Black art. As a Black woman, she appears to Reuel and requests his assistance; Reuel interprets her desire for help as a desire for inclusion in dominant white society, although her alignment with blackness should suggest her comfort with and commitment to remaining excluded. Instead, he "helps" her by denying her blackness and transforming her into a white woman, giving her access and inclusion into dominant culture. Readers may interpret Dianthe's request for assistance as an attempt to convince Reuel to acknowledge his own identity and to join her in valuing blackness. bell hooks states that "loving blackness as political resistance transforms our ways of looking and being, and thus creates the conditions necessary for us to move against the forces of domination and death and reclaim black life" (Hooks, *Black Looks*, 32). Thus we may view Dianthe's pre-amnesia state, one of valuing blackness in the face of white domination, as a strong political stance of empowerment. But Reuel's response to Dianthe shows that in the domestic version of the Black nation novel, especially around the turn-of-the-twentieth-century, it is difficult to love blackness if one seeks the middle class attainment of success prevalent in dominant society.

Another view of Dianthe's attempts at empowerment through claiming blackness can be seen in her experience with Aunt Hannah. After being educated in the truth of her identity, and under Aunt Hannah's distinctively Black influence, Dianthe no longer values whiteness over blackness and attempts to remove from her life the person who is representative of the white power structure—Aubrey. Knowing that she has been forced into a sexual and incestuous relationship with both of her brothers, she attempts, though without success, to poison Aubrey. Dianthe fails because Aubrey, privy to the same mystical powers as Reuel and Dianthe, envisions her plan before she can ennact it. Hopkins's presentation of Aubrey, as a white male appropriating the talents that are specifically Black, is a critique of the dominant culture's appropriation of that which is valuable in the African American community (spirituality, Black womanhood, history). By exploiting these talents, Aubrey is able to use them against the community from which they originated; thus Hopkins completes the portrait of her despair over the possibility of a domestic Black nation.

Spirituality, Secrecy, and Global Nation Building

After thus critiquing the effectiveness of domestic Black nation politics—the desire for inclusion into a North American society grounded in white supremacy and the legacy of plantation slavery—Hopkins promotes a global approach to nation building through Reuel's ultimately positive experience on his expedition. But although Reuel's African journey is meant by Aubrey to be a death trip, it is in Africa that he becomes fully alive. Both Reuel and Dianthe are emotionally dead as Reuel begins his trip because they have no acceptable heritage to acknowledge; Reuel acknowledges spirituality and mysticism, but does not accredit it to his blackness. Reuel's first glimpse of Africa initiates a new connection with blackness: "as there is an intimate relation between the character of a country and that of its people, Reuel realized vividly that the race who dwelt here must be different from those of the rest of the world" (509). Although he does not understand of what this difference consists, Reuel sees beauty in the land and the people.

Reuel is separated from Dianthe by distance while in Ethiopia and receives news from Aubrey of her death. This final separation propels Reuel into "community" work. Reuel's connection to domestic quests of inclusion is severed with Dianthe's "death" and he is freed, just as Blake, Belton, and Bernard were freed in previous novels by the absence of the women they loved, to pursue the success and progress of the Black community as a whole. Within the Black nation novel, race leaders, and thus far all the race leaders are male, are prevented from pursuing nation building when they are involved in the securing of a home on domestic soil. Securing a Black home, which includes marriage, entails protecting Black womanhood, but also pursuing inclusion into dominant society. Because dominant society excludes blackness, this quest is ongoing and futile. So it should be no surprise that with Dianthe's death, Reuel begins to acknowledge his connection and responsibility to blackness and the Black community.

By creating Telassar, a successful, productive Black nation, protected from the corrupting influences of whiteness, and exploring Reuel's connection to it, Hopkins effectively dismisses the American plantation system, as well as the ideologies of assimilation and racial uplift. Although Reuel embarks upon his expedition thinking of it in quintessentially American terms as a treasure hunt, what he finds instead is his own positive African history, something quite different from what he has been running away. The possibility of Ethiopian greatness predating Egyptian civilization—under the pyramids—threatens the power structure of white over Black in the United States. Hopkins recognizes "Anglo-Saxon" resistance to fact, which undermine their favorite theories, but she is more concerned here with the transformation within the African American community following the demonstration of this theory in the city of Telassar. Such a discovery shifts no power unless the African American community connects with this positive history. Professor Stone explains, "Undoubtedly your Afro-Americans are a branch of the wonderful and mysterious Ethiopians who had prehistoric existence of magnificence the full record of which is lost in obscurity" (532). This connection of the African American to this group of "civilized" Africans is shocking to Charlie, who remarks, in response, "Great Scott! ...you don't mean to tell me that all this was done by *niggers*?" (532). His comment reinforces the necessity in seeking a homeplace and building a nation outside of the United States; on domestic soil blackness will always be seen as negative and inferior by dominant society, while in a global context, blackness flourishes and is validated. Moreover, the mark of blackness, as represented on Reuel (as well as on Aubrey and Dianthe) in the form of a lotus-lily birthmark upon the breast, which he is determined to keep hidden, is the very mark, which allows him inclusion to such a history.

Reuel's despondency over what he believes to be Dianthe's death leads him to initially contemplate suicide indicating his inability to see another option; he knows of no other place to seek inclusion and therefore he is emotionally lost. It is at this point that he stumbles upon the lost city of Telassar. This accidental discovery "was but the re-awakening of life within him" (543). In that lost city Hopkins recreates a multicolored community, with which Reuel and the reader are already familiar. Earlier in the novel we met the Fisk Jubilee Singers, celebrating blackness, who range "from alabaster to ebony" (451). Similarly, the inhabitants of

Telassar "ranged in complexion from a creamy tint to purest ebony; the long hair...varied in texture from soft, waving curls to the crispness of the most pronounce African type" (545). While the one-drop rule forces exclusion from American society (one drop of African blood that is), Telassar, representing a global Black nation, does not exclude, regardless of white "impurity." The change in Reuel is significant: "Upon Reuel a strange force seemed working. If what he heard was true, how great a destiny was his!...He felt keenly now the fact that he had played the coward's part in hiding his origin" (558, 560). His transformation, expressed as a decision to reject assimilation, comes from his acceptance of blackness as valuable. With this transformation, he is acknowledged as the royalty the Telessars have awaited and he is greeted with, "Thou art Ergamenes—the long-looked-for king of Ethiopia, for whose reception this city was built!" (554).

In Telassar Reuel finds a civilization that values, protects, and respects Black womanhood, as he is told by his guide, Ai:

> We are a singular people, governed by a female monarch, all having the same name, Candace, and a Council of twenty-five Sages, who are educated for periodical visits to the outer world. Queen Candace is a virgin queen who waits the coming of Ergamenes to inaugurate a dynasty of kings. Our virgins live within the inner city, and from among them Candace chooses her successor at intervals of fifteen years. (561)

Upon meeting Queen Candace, Reuel is reminded of Dianthe, only in bronzed form; here Hopkins suggests the possibility of Dianthe's own sacredness, and that of African American womanhood in general, which has been desecrated while seeking inclusion through the African American community's inability to protect Black womanhood from white male lust within a society of white supremacy. When the novel takes a global focus, outside the constraints of the U.S. nation-state, Hopkins reconstructs a Black nation that centers the Black woman and is based on a spiritual foundation and not material success.

Ai, Reuel's mediator between the world of Telassar that he must come to accept and the Western thought he must leave behind, understands both worlds. Ai acts as guide whose responsibility it is to transform Reuel from a person who has denied blackness in order to be accepted by a society of white supremacy, into a productive member of a community that values and praises blackness. He also explains the responsibility Reuel must accept in becoming a member of this community: restoration. Telassar is waiting "for the coming of our king who shall restore...Destroyed and abased because of her idolatries, Ethiopia's arrogance" (547). The previous destruction of Telassar, which may also be seen as the destruction of the global African community, is attributed to "her [Telassar's] idolatries." In a vision, Dianthe questions Reuel, "Why did you leave me in the power of a fiend in human shape, to search for gold? There are worse things in life than poverty" (579). The interpretation of the destruction and abasement of Ethiopia as divine retribution for idolatry parallels African Americans' own idolatry of a system that seeks every means to exclude them.

Telassar's faith in future redemption is presented as the fulfillment of biblical prophecy, as Ai explains to Reuel, "a hope held out to the faithful worshippers of the true God that Ethiopia should stretch forth her hand unto Eternal Goodness, and that then her glory should again dazzle the world" (548). First, it is important to note that Hopkins gives the Ethiopian (and therefore African) the voice of the Christian biblical verse, Psalm 68:31, thus refuting previous notions of African heathenism. Moreover, that which shall redeem Ethiopia, should also redeem the African American community:

> By divine revelation David beheld the present time, when, after Christ's travail for the sins of humanity, the time of Ethiopia's atonement being past, purged of idolatry, accepting the One Only God through His Son

> Jesus, suddenly should come a new birth to the
> descendants of Ham, and Ethiopia should return to her
> ancient glory! Ergamenes, all hail! (558-559)

The community of Telassar, although secluded, accepts
Christianity as a means of atonement and redemption. Their
acceptance of the Hamatic myth includes African Americans
and those of African descent within the Diaspora who have
been enslaved in the process of Ethiopian redemption.

Reuel's access to the royal destiny comes from the
bloodline of his mother, Mira. She bears the lotus flower
birthmark and passes this lineage to all of her children. This
royal status contrasts greatly with the inferior status that is
passed from the Black mother to her children in the United
States under slavery. When pursuing inclusion into
dominant society, one must often reject one's unvalued
Black mother to succeed; but in the global nation, one
celebrates the Black mother in order to reap the rewards of
inheritance. Hopkins also presents the Black mother as
bestowing the talents of mysticism, seen as a part of an
Ethiopian spirituality, and Reuel must also recognize this
connection:

> From her [his mother] he had inherited his mysticism
> and his occult powers. The nature of the mystic within
> him was, then, but a dreamlike devotion of the spirit
> that had swayed his ancestors, it was the shadow of
> Ethiopia's power. (558)

Reuel had tapped into this power a few times but he had not
fully accepted or acknowledged what it meant. Dianthe and
Aubrey also had this talent, also being Mira's children.
Dianthe cannot take full advantage of this power due to her
amnesia regarding her blackness, and Aubrey only uses his
powers against the Black community.

"All of one blood" concerns not only Black and white,
but more specifically a connection between Reuel, Aubrey,
and Dianthe which is finally revealed. With the knowledge
that they are all siblings, Reuel makes his final break with
the quest for inclusion: "And Reuel cursed with a mighty

curse the bond that bound him to the white race of his native land" (594). The sibling relationship between the three was created by white male abuse of Black womanhood. The incestuous relationship between the three can be seen as a remnant of white supremacy's devaluing of blackness: Aunt Hannah conceives Mira through a relationship with the first Livingston; Mira conceives Reuel, Dianthe, and Aubrey through a relationship with the second Livingston, her own half brother; and in passing for white, Reuel and Aubrey attempt to recreate, with their sister, the incestuous relationship of their parents. The brothers and sister all suffer the consequences of "passing" by variously enduring shame, melancholy, amnesia, and/or suicide. Passing, presented by Hopkins as amnesia (Dianthe), melancholy (Reuel), and psycho-pathology (Aubrey), is treated in a more modern and pathological way than it had been by earlier writers; her views are not unlike Griggs's presentation of the psychology of assimilation as masochism. At the same time, Hopkins discusses the dangers of assimilation to Black life in the United States in terms that recall Delany's antebellum commentary on the vulnerability of Black families. Because Aubrey and Dianthe are unaware of and/or ashamed of their African heritage, they cannot reap its royal benefits. Although Reuel, Aubrey, and Dianthe are all of one blood, it is assumed that only Reuel receives and accepts a psychological transformation and experiences empowerment due to his direct experience with a positive ancient African history and culture.

The ultimate marriage of Reuel and Candace suggests the utopian possibility of a relationship of equals between the Black man and woman, forming a strong foundation for the global Black nation. Although Telassar retains its queen, it searches for its king; it has been governed by a female, suggesting matriarchal rule, but its success will come from a partnership: "You, Ergamenes, shall begin the restoration of Ethiopia" (555). It is important to note that although the Ethiopians have secluded themselves away from whiteness, it is still Westernness in Reuel that will help provide redemption to the community. Much like Delany's belief in the ability of the African American to restore Africa, Reuel brings with him the positive qualities of the West without the destructive impulse of the white community.

Blackness and Nation Building

Although it is Dianthe's blackness to which both Aubrey and Reuel are attracted and feel the need to possess, it is this same blackness that both force her to hide. Thus, the Black woman is sexually exploited and silenced in the domestic Black nation by the white male power structure, but also by the Black male because of his collusion with the white male power structure as a being seeking inclusion. By contrast, in the global nation the Black woman is empowered by the sacred and protected position that the Black male (and the community) places her in. Moreover, while Reuel must hide his own as well as his wife/sister's blackness when subscribing to domestic Black nation ideology, once he accepts and becomes enmeshed in a global vision, Reuel marries Candace, a visibly Black woman. This act transcends his previous belief in the domestic nation of having to transform Dianthe into a white woman in order to marry her.

And finally, whereas Dianthe's plot to kill Aubrey fails, perhaps because her new found blackness is without a strong historical foundation to combat the white supremacy it faces, Reuel returns to the United States with the historical awareness Dianthe lacks. The reader assumes that Aubrey is made privy to his own racial history: "He was changed and his auburn locks were prematurely grey. His eyes revealed an impenetrable mystery within into whose secret depths no mortal eye might look" (619). Instead of seeking justice for the death of Dianthe through legal means, Ai, by order of Reuel, places Aubrey under hypnotic influence to kill himself. Aubrey's death is seen as a greater act of justice than any court system could provide, as he suffers "death by thine own hand" (620). Hopkins suggests, still, as Aubrey represents white male dominance, that justice for crimes committed against the African American community will be carried out through a strengthening of Black value. Such episodes suggest that Hopkins is not calling for a physical emigration to Africa, as Delany once did, but more of an emigration of the mind—an alignment with blackness which racial uplift and assimilation do not promote.

Hopkins, expanding on Delany's critique of a domestic Black nation and on the great possibilities of a global Black nation, also utilizes a divided plot line in *Of One Blood*. But unlike Delany, Hopkins expands on the vulnerable position of the Black woman in the domestic context, critiquing the ways in which the Black man participates in the demise of the Black woman by seeking inclusion and thereby colluding with dominant society in the devaluing of Black womanhood. Similar to Griggs, Hopkins also critiques racial uplift as a viable strategy for inclusion; but unlike Griggs, she offers a more concrete, although not complete, dismissal of the possibility of a separate Black nation on domestic soil, due to the lack of a safe space for the Black woman. Although both Delany and Griggs end their novels with no complete imagining of a solution, Hopkins comes closer to presenting a community that values blackness and Black womanhood. Her success in doing this comes from her willingness to situate a nation outside the confines of Western thought and influence: Telassar as an underground and secret place. Although Delany, Griggs, and Hopkins all accept Christianity as the spiritual foundation for redemption, Hopkins, like Delany, does not present it as a strictly Western religion; the people of Telassar prior to Reuel's "return" already subscribe to certain attributes of Christianity—the Trinity, Christ, biblical scripture—and therefore, for Hopkins, Christianity escapes its previous negative and too pacific undertones.

Thus she refines Delany's use of spirituality in Black nation formation.

Hopkins also differs from Delany and Griggs by imagining a global Black nation that values and empowers Black women, produces healthy Black homes, and calls for successful unions between Black men and women in nation building. Such a treatment is missing from both of the previous Black nation novels. Although Hopkins echoes Delany and his fictional treatment of Africa, her return to Africa is figurative and ideological more than it is literal and physical. Hopkins is not only calling for a physical emigration to Africa, as Delany once did, but for an emigration of the mind—an alignment with blackness which racial uplift and assimilation do not promote. In this regard Hopkins is an important bridge connecting Delany with Du Bois, the next author to be explored in the Black nation novel tradition.

W.E.B. Du Bois, the Folk, and Racial Uplift in *The Quest of the Silver Fleece*

Freedom is a state of mind: a spiritual unchoking of the wells of human power and superhuman love.

—W.E.B. Du Bois

In 1903, W.E.B. Du Bois published *The Souls of Black Folk*[1] a collection of essays which propelled him into the position of race leader; many regard this as his greatest work, and it is certainly his best known. David Levering Lewis, in *W.E.B. Du Bois: Biography of a Race, 1868-1919* (1993), claims that the book:

> ...redefined the terms of a three-hundred-year interaction between black and white people and influenced the cultural and political psychology of peoples of African descent throughout the Western hemisphere, as well as on the continent of Africa. (277)

In the first essay of the collection, "Of Our Spiritual Strivings," Du Bois advances ideas of African Americans as a people with a valuable history and culture of their own, having made contributions to the world as great as Europeans. But most significantly, in this collection Du Bois identifies the "double consciousness" operating within the African American:

> It is a peculiar sensation, this double consciousness, this sense of always looking at one's self through the eyes of others, of measuring one's soul by the tape of a world that looks on in amused contempt and pity. One ever feels his two-ness, — an American, a Negro; two souls, two thoughts, two unreconciled strivings; two warring ideals in one dark body, whose dogged strength alone keeps it from being torn asunder. (38)

Du Bois not only identifies this twoness but also celebrates it as a gift. What he critiques is the inability, due to white supremacy, to incorporate this gift with the pursuit of citizenship in the United States:

> The history of the American Negro is the history of this strife, — this longing to attain self-conscious manhood, to merge his double self into a better and truer self. ...he simply wishes to make it possible for a man to be both a Negro and an American, without being cursed and spit upon by his fellows, without having the doors of Opportunity closed roughly in his face. (39)

In *Souls* Du Bois presents a dichotomy between being American and being Negro, his desire to heal this split with the efforts that I recognize as racial uplift, as well as other issues Du Bois recognizes as specific to the African American community and examines how he, along with Martin Delany, Sutton Griggs, and Pauline Hopkins, turned to fiction in an attempt to imagine a community which implemented his theories on race, inclusion and exclusion. Du Bois's commitment to racial uplift responds to Delany's call for a domestic solution through the novel *The Quest for the Silver Fleece* (1911).[2] In *Quest*, Du Bois extends the examinations of a domestic solution offered by Delany and Griggs, but also furthers the discussion of gender inclusion begun by Hopkins. Like the previous authors, Du Bois also connects a commitment and foundation based on valuing blackness as pertinent to the construction of a healthy Black domestic nation; moreover, he critiques assimilation and adoption of white American values as a viable strategy for Black communal success.

Quest defies neat categorization. It is often compared to Frank Norris's wheat novels, *The Octopus* (1901) and *The Pit* (1903), because of Du Bois's use of the cotton crop as a thread which unifies all the characters of the novel. This connection with Norris often leads to a treatment of *Quest* as a naturalist text. Such a treatment frustrates, though, because the novel insists on a romantic ending, instead of the usual pessimistic conclusion one would typically expect to find in naturalist prose. Also, Du Bois explores the political and economic manipulations of those in power, suggesting that oppressive conditions are not, as naturalism would have it, determined by fate, destiny, or divine forces, but rather by human will. Bernard Bell, in *The Afro-American Novel and Its Tradition* (1987), in examining *Quest* as a case of resistance to the naturalist form, states, "The sociohistorical source of this tension [between Du Bois and a naturalist aesthetic] is the deep-rooted romantic belief of nineteenth century black Americans in moral responsibility and free will, in a world of purpose and meaning, which contradicted deterministic philosophy and mechanistic despair" (81). Another trend in the critical reception of *Quest* is to see the novel as an economic and political treatise. Here the emphasis is on Du Bois's indictment of the sharecropping and penal systems as extensions of slavery and not causes of the inferior position in which the African American community finds itself. Critics of this type see Du Bois promoting a strategy for Black success grounded in financial independence through the cotton crop and "uplifting" the swamp through education.

Quest, although not usually noted for any literary merit, is seen as historically important in the African American literary tradition. It stands as one of only two novels—along with James Weldon Johnson's *The Autobiography of an Ex-Coloured Man* (1912)—still read that were published between two booming eras, the turn of the twentieth century and the Harlem Renaissance/New Negro Movement.[3] Both novels explore double consciousness of their African American characters and the desire and quest for inclusion into dominant society. But where Johnson's character succeeds in reaching inclusion by passing, only to realize by the end of his life that he has given up something important—blackness, Du Bois's characters come to reaffirm blackness as an important foundation for success and they decide to forego inclusion for greater community progress.

Arnold Rampersad, in *The Art and Imagination of W.E.B. Du Bois* (1976), has to date given the most serious examination of Du Bois as a fiction writer. Unlike other critics, Rampersad recognizes *Quest* as "first, a simple love story" (117). Although he addresses political and economic issues in the novel, calling *Quest* "the first piece of Afro-American fiction to include a serious study of economic forces among the basic factors determining the quality of black American life" (132), he also calls attention to the character of Bles as a personification of Du Bois's theory of the African American divided self. For Rampersad, Bles is not divided as an American and a Negro, the two warring souls Du Bois identifies in *Souls*. Instead, Rampersad identifies Bles's division as "the Puritan or Calvinist conscience…'grafted' on a tropical body and temperament. …Its effect, unlike that of the American souls at war with its African counterpart, is always positive and constructive as a force for moral and psychological discrimination" (123). Rampersad sees Du Bois's first examination of Talented Tenth leadership as the necessary link to uplift the community.

My examination of *Quest* moves in a different direction than previous critiques. Unlike Rampersad, I recognize in the novel a questioning by Du Bois of his own theories of Talented Tenth leadership and racial uplift as a means toward achieving full citizenship for the African American. I see Du Bois celebrating, as he first did in *Souls*, the talents found in the folk community, and the equal exchange that should take place between the folk and the talented tenth. Also, Du Bois's novel is the first that explores the fitness of Black women for leadership roles and advocated their inclusion. Moreover, *Quest* responds to previous calls from Delany and Griggs for a domestic solution to the exclusion of African Americans from the nation of their birth. Du Bois is more optimistic than Delany or Griggs in his imagining of the possibility of a domestic solution, perhaps because of his commitment to racial uplift. But unlike Du Bois's previous calls for integration, in the novel he identifies the swamp as a separate Black community that can become a thriving locale only by remaining separate and relying on Black leadership. The novel is optimistic in imagining the possibility of Black liberation without violence, but pessimistic in its outlook in imagining a community separate and not integrated. The secret to success in *Quest* is relying on Black leadership who have been educated by the dominant society (racial uplift) but do not value dominant ideals, include Black women as leaders and retain a strong sense of blackness as valuable. Situating *Quest* within the paradigm of Black nation novels re-orients our sense of the ideological content of this novel and allows us to extract a much more nuanced awareness of the relationship between Du Bois's art and his politics.

The main characters in the plot of *Quest* fit into stereotypes in order to make a larger statement regarding the ways in which America responds to race. Bles and Zora represent typical groups within the African American community: those seeking inclusion and those comfortable with exclusion. Elspeth, Zora's mother, represents that part of the community most connected to African roots (through language, spirituality, and land) but corrupted by white America; Elspeth assists in "selling" Black womanhood to white male lust. There is potential in Elspeth, as her connection to what is considered African is seen as powerful, but she is also dangerous to the foundation of a Black nation. Despite a humble and "immoral" beginning—born in the swamp, with Elspeth for a mother, her chastity stolen before she even understood its value, and uneducated in the formal sense—Zora shows promise because of her survivor's spirit, her commitment to and love of blackness, and her consistent positive attitude. She represents, for Du Bois, the masses of the African American community to whom the gifts of blackness are given.[4]

The Swamp and the Black Woman in Domestic Nation Building

In *Quest*, Du Bois locates the possible domestic Black nation in the swamp of the South's black belt (in Alabama). The reader is introduced to this place while also first seeing our protagonists Zora and Bles, who have opposite responses to the swamp. Bles, already deep in the process of becoming "uplifted," sees the swamp as "sinister and sullen" (13). The swamp is full of vegetation, water, colors, feelings, spirits, and music: the latter of which he recognizes as "a human music, but of a wildness and a weirdness" (14). Bles, having stumbled upon the swamp while lost on his way to boarding school, feels fear instead of security in this possible homeplace. The primitiveness of the swamp contrasts with the refinement he is striving towards through education; his uplift process, although incomplete at this time, has already served to separate him from a distinctive cultural blackness represented in the swamp. Yet although Bles feels no positive connection to the land, he is stirred by the sight of Zora: "Amid this mighty halo, as on clouds of flame, a girl was dancing" (14). Zora, unlike Bles, finds personal and pure pleasure in connecting with the swamp; moreover, she is a personification of the swamp, and because of this, he is drawn to her, much in the same way we see Reuel drawn to Dianethe's blackness in *Of One Blood*. Du Bois suggests Bles's ability (and the ability of those that have separated themselves from the masses) to return to blackness despite his commitment to racial uplift, which remains a conflict for him throughout the novel.

Zora is also able to vocalize the essence of the swamp as blackness. She says to the fearful Bles, "Who's afeared of the dark? I love night" (17). Du Bois's use of Zora, as a brown skinned African American woman, breaks with the traditional use of a mulatta, quadroon, octoroon, or just light-skinned female protagonist which populate most of the antebellum and postbellum fiction prior to *Quest*. Griggs uses brown skinned female characters in *Imperium* (Antoinette and Viola) but neither is given the degree of importance Du Bois offers Zora. Zora's declarative statement—"I love night"—is equivalent to Langston Hughes's celebration of blackness,[5] to the "Black is Beautiful" movement, and the political affirmation of the 1960s Civil Rights and Black Arts Movements. In addition, Zora brings to the swamp, and to Bles, an understanding of the ancient continuum of blackness, perhaps regardless of location, by stating "We'se know us all our lives, and—before, ain't we?" (18). This suggests that Bles's history (both personal and as a representative of the Talented Tenth) is located in the swamp and before the swamp—pre-North America. Although she originates from the swamp, Zora links herself to Bles easily and immediately; whereas racial uplift has disconnected Bles from the swamp, Zora's foundation of blackness (the swamp) serves to reconnect those of the community that may have temporarily been lost.

While Bles is "brainwashed" by education, Zora is more skeptical of his path:

> They [white people] don't really rule; they just thinks they rule. They just got things,—heavy dead things. We black folks is got the spirit.... Black folks is wonderful. (46)

Here Zora attempts to privilege the talents of the Black community over what Bles values in the white community. She also questions the idea that power stems from material possessions, which have no life; more powerful than the material, for Zora, is what she calls the spirit. Zora recognizes in the Black community an emotion and connection to a higher power that is missing in the white community. This comparison causes Zora to view her own community as superior, an interpretation that Bles is unable to accept. Here Du Bois responds to the calls of the previous authors in this study for a redefined spirituality as the foundation of an imagined Black nation. Although Zora can not yet articulate what she means by the spirit, she is connected to a worshipping of the land and to non-Christian rituals to which Bles is not privy.

Also unlike Bles, Zora is able to keep a healthy perspective; she sees the danger in people like Mary Taylor and the Cresswells. Her gift, this second sight, she attributes to her connection to her community, and she explains to Bles, "I can see right through people. You can't. You never had a witch for a mammy—did you" (46). Knowing Bles's limitations and lack of "second sight," Zora still submits to his demands that she "conform" her wild ways and join him at the school because she desires a connection to him. She becomes partially convinced there may be some value in education and is willing to give it a try. Bles assumes that racial uplift means the rejection of one's humble beginnings and assures her, "When you're educated you won't want to live in the swamp" (50). He desires Zora's energy but is not willing in the first part of the novel to accept the negative connotations that come along with her history. Zora, on the other hand, is willing to recognize some value in education and racial uplift, but also understands that a complete conversion means the loss of positive aspects found in her community. Instead she compromises, "I don't want to board in—I wants to be free" (51). The act of boarding in at Miss Smith's school, a complete acceptance of white superiority and assimilation, is akin to slavery for Zora, voluntarily removing oneself from all that is familiar and choosing to live in a potentially hostile environment.

While Zora is representative of the positive qualities of the swamp, a homeplace centered in that part of blackness which assimilationists (which we see from Bles's reaction) find disturbing and embarrassing, Du Bois complicates the image of this possible homeplace by including in it Elspeth, Zora's mother, an imposing and evil figure.[6] Upon Elspeth's entrance into the swamp, Bles is once again afraid and alone, as Zora has disappeared. Zora instinctively knows that she must remove herself from dangerous situations, fleeing before Elspeth finds her. Bles, unaware of what should be acknowledged as a threat, remains in Elspeth's presence and retains his original fear of the swamp. Through the reactions of these three characters, Du Bois presents the swamp not as a utopia but as a place with potential, presenting whatever image is imposed upon it: good (Zora), bad (Elspeth), or indifferent (Bles).

Bles represents that part of the Black community desperately searching for a place of belonging. He comes from out of state (Georgia) in order to attend school. He speaks nothing of a family left behind; he is the motherless child, and as such, he quickly and eagerly adopts the attitudes of racial uplift. He believes in education and sexual purity as the paths to inclusion by the dominant society. Although he is drawn to Zora and what she represents, he is not fully accepting of her because she is not acceptable to white society, and it is because of this that he attempts to change her. Bles represents that part of the community that Du Bois labels as "The Talented Tenth," educated and responsible for presenting to the dominant society the humanity of the African American community as well as lifting up the masses "beneath" them. Yet Du Bois also presents Bles as "needing" Zora, rather than Zora needing Bles, which examines the Black elite's dependence on remaining connected to the Black community in order to be a part of community success, instead of seeking only individual progress.

In contrast to the swamp is Miss Smith's school for Negro children, where African Americans are "prepared" to take their place in a new world. Her program of education and uplift consists of removing traces of the swamp from her students and preparing them to enter dominant white society. It is important that Du Bois places Bles's first experience in Alabama not at the school with Miss Smith but in the swamp with Zora. The education and racial uplift program is an attractive route towards possible inclusion into the larger domestic nation (the U.S.), but Du Bois critiques it as a process that may separate the Black intellectual (the Talented Tenth) from his Black community. On the other hand, a separate Black domestic nation, represented as the swamp, within a larger nation is vulnerable to oppression without the leadership that comes through education and racial uplift.

Just as Du Bois is careful not to present the swamp as a utopia, neither is the school a haven for African Americans. Mary Taylor, a New England teacher come to Alabama, is discouraged with her first teaching opportunity in Miss Smith's Negro school, although she considers herself a supporter of equal rights. Clearly politically different than Miss Smith, Mary Taylor is a threat to the utopian possibilities of the school because she does not fully believe in the potential for Black uplift. Yet, Mary's ability to communicate and have a positive experience with Bles, despite the color line, is a testament to Du Bois's idea of the success of the Talented Tenth on the white community. Bles's ability to converse with Mary on an educated level contradicts whatever negative stereotypes she may have regarding Black people, or Black men specifically. Although Mary is able to "see past" Bles's color and the negative connotations it represents in society, she is unable to transfer her attitude toward him onto the larger Black community, but instead views Bles as an exception; if Bles is an exceptional Black man, Mary is able to see beyond his color, accept him as an equal (or close to equal), and yet continue to subscribe to her racist attitude that the Black community as a whole is inferior and savage. This is clearly seen through her condescension toward Zora throughout most of the novel, as Zora is representative of the masses moving into the "New Negro" and not the Talented Tenth. Du Bois critiques the practicality of racial uplift as a program to create large changes in the dominant society by showing that as Mary's interest in Bles grows, so does her criticism of and displeasure in Zora.

The African American inner struggle, examined in all the novels in this study, between pursuing a quest for inclusion, separating from dominant society, and committing to valuing blackness is presented through an unusual "love triangle" of Bles, Mary and Zora, with the two women vying for the attention and affection of Bles. Mary represents inclusion and acceptance by dominant society, whereas Zora represents a separatist outlook. Zora instantly recognizes the situation as one of conflict and boldly states her displeasure to her competitor when she sees Mary and Bles in a carriage one day: "I hates you" (43). Mary, because she is not honest with herself, as well as ignorant of the repercussions of her actions on others, is less direct in her attack on Zora, resorting to comments such as, "She is a bold, godless thing" (67). The reader sees that Bles is caught between assimilation and separation—Mary representing the former, Zora the latter. Because Zora is so resistant to "conforming" and so secure in her love of blackness, Bles, as well as Mary, sees her as an other—a godless thing:

> [Mary] looked at Zora disapprovingly, while Zora looked at her quite impersonally, but steadily. Then Miss Taylor braced herself, mentally, and took the war into Africa. (71)

While Mary sees in Zora the Dark Continent that must be tamed and conquered, Zora is representative for the reader of the pre-slavery spirit the community must regain; a spirit that stands as an equal when confronted with racist ideology.

Zora's resistance to dominant ideas about blackness is also revealed through her interactions with Mary Taylor. Unlike Miss Smith, Mary believes dominant society must educate African Americans only to create better servants. In an attempt to convince Zora to aspire to be a maid or cook, she insists, "Zora, your people must learn to work and work steadily and work hard—"(73). Zora, in response, remains defiant regarding the superiority of the Black community even in the face of white power [Mary], offering her own definition of the African American community:

> Do you know my people? They don't work; they plays. They is all little funny, dark people. They flies and creeps and crawls, slippery-like; and they cries and calls. Ah, my people! my poor little people! They misses me these days, because they is shadowy things that sing and smell and bloom in dark and terrible nights. (74)

Zora's description, although mysterious, is not meant to educate Mary about the Black/swamp community; its purpose is to reveal that Mary is ignorant of the people she assumes to know how to help. Zora, I believe, signifies on Mary's assumed superiority and education due to her privileged status as a white woman.[8] Mary's solution for the Black community is more hard work (i.e. a new slavery), revealing her ignorance about political and economic oppression as well as her racist views on the laziness of the community. Zora's answer defines her community as more than slaves and servants, and attributes to them talents and skills beyond the imagination of white America. She also acknowledges the pain of separation she feels from having submitted to the program of education. Earlier, she confessed, "I don't work; mostly I dreams. But I can work, and I will—for the wonder things—and for you [Bles]" (49). Her desire to dream instead of work speaks to her survival spirit, as dreaming is characteristic of a hopeful nature; her dreams allow her to remain independent of assimilation strategies. Zora's willingness to work "for the wonder things" indicates that her energy is saved for plans independent of the white community; willingness to work for Bles shows a commitment to the members of the Black community.

Planning the Domestic Black Nation

Although Du Bois presents Zora as emotionally stronger than Bles, especially in the face of white supremacy, when they work together they are most effective. With his formal education, Bles is able to make larger political connections regarding race relations. Upon learning the story of Jason and the Golden Fleece, he relates Jason to the Cresswells—both he views as thieves—and the slave cabins to the Black Sea. When Bles retells the tale to Zora, she is able to interpret Elspeth as the character of the witch. Together they are capable of making plans of harvesting their own crop of silver fleece; Bles provides the management (the plan) and Zora provides the raw material (access to the swamp and the magical seed from Elspeth). Through this collaboration, Du Bois presents a productive foundation for an imagined domestic Black nation—the unification of the Talented Tenth and the masses towards some autonomous program for Black liberation. Moreover, the imagining of such a foundation connects Du Bois with the other authors in this study, as well as places *Quest* in the genre of the "Black nation novel" as all four authors have suggested that the African American's contribution to the Black nation (whether domestic or global) should be one of intelligence and understanding of the workings of power, while the contribution of the African masses shall be labor.[9]

The seed Elspeth describes is a "wonder seed, sowed wid the three spells of Obi in the old land ten thousand moons ago. But you couldn't plan it, it would kill you" (75). Du Bois suggests that the saving future for the Black community, represented as the seed, must come out of the past, that part of the community that is uncorrupted by white "civilization"; because of the seed's "purity," it is seen as too powerful for those removed from the source. Although Elspeth "owns" the seed, she has not planted it. The transfer of seed from Elspeth to Bles and Zora transfers power from the old Negro, compliant with white supremacy, to the New Negro and the Talented Tenth. Zora's desire to plant the seed in a secret place in the swamp connects the novel to the other texts in this study and suggests Du Bois's concurrence with the call for secrecy in the forming of the Black nation, initiated by Delany with the secret revolutionary organization, and repeated by Griggs with the Imperium and Hopkins with the city of Telassar. Bles's objection to secrecy is a dangerous habit for an oppressed minority group seeking a revolutionary change of circumstance. Zora's understanding of secrecy connects her character with other leaders of imagined Black nations in this study (Blake, Bernard and Belton, Reuel, and Princess Kautilya).

Zora keeps secret the location of the special land, the secret place in the swamp, described as "a long island . . . the soil was virgin and black," and in doing so is protecting what is Black and valuable; a place to nurture the dream of Zora and Bles (the silver fleece they plan to grow will be their means to financial independence) (78). The reader, thinking of *Blake, Imperium*, and *Of One Blood*, can interpret this place as representative of Black womanhood, which must be secluded, protected, and pure in order to bear "magical" fruit. Zora's secrecy regarding this place, and later her complete commitment to nurturing and working the crop, symbolizes her new concern for nurturing her own body. Having lost her chastity, which should have been secreted and protected, at the hands of the Cresswells, her dreams of individual success are now transferred to the silver fleece, as she hopes this magical crop will make up for her own deficiencies. For it is only after Bles and Zora plant the seed that she decides to board at the school, leaving Elspeth's home and removing her body from the access of the Cresswells. Zora's budding womanhood (both her physical being and the symbolic silver fleece) is then allowed to develop, not through racial uplift, but through a nurturing

119

safe environment away from white male lust and oppression. Black womanhood is not described as an imitation of white or true womanhood (piety, purity, domesticity, and submissiveness), but as something more spiritual, political, and natural. Moreover, Black womanhood here is connected to the future success of the Black nation in the prediction that Zora (and Black women like her) will be central to a healthy black nation:

> She would, unhindered, develop to a brilliant, sumptuous womanhood; proud, conquering, full-blooded, and deep-bosomed—a passionate mother of men. (125)

Du Bois agrees with the previous calls to make the family the foundation of the Black nation, but he is more progressive than earlier writers in suggesting that such a foundation can still develop out of what was previously seen as tainted.

As Zora and Bles wait for the harvest of their cotton crop, the catalyst for radical change in the swamp, Bles recognizes that the racial uplift program in which he has convinced Zora to participate is changing them both. Bles believed that education, even in this racist world, would provide opportunities for him despite his blackness, but as he develops his skills he sees few opportunities to use his education. Here Du Bois critiques the nation's unwillingness to accept a Black elite community outside of the parameters of service and manual labor. His critique parallels that in Griggs's *Imperium,* where the character of Belton is unable to find employment appropriate to his education level and must resort to working as a maid in drag. As he questions his own progress through racial uplift, Bles also questions the results of his convincing Zora to conform:

> She was drifting away from him in some intangible way to an upper world of dress and language and deportment, and the new thought was pain to him. (128)

In conforming to a white value system and rejecting her original state, Zora gives up the very things that drew Bles to her, ultimately destroying the very thing Bles initially desired. Moreover, although Bles at first thinks it will be desirable, the separation of the masses (Zora's old ways) from the elite (Bles), becomes painful in actuality.

Zora for a time conforms to the type of womanhood expected of her through racial uplift, silencing those aspects of blackness that first attracted Bles. Yet despite this transformation, Bles ultimately rejects Zora upon learning of her sexual impurity, or rather, learning that she continues to live despite the loss of her chastity. Walking hand in hand along the road, Zora and Bles are verbally assaulted by Harry Cresswell who labels Zora as "notorious" (166). His epithet drives a wedge between the young lovers:

> On the lovers the words fell like a blow. Zora shivered, and a grayish horror mottled the dark burning of her face. Bles started in anger, then paused in shivering doubt. What had happened? They knew not; yet involuntarily their hands fell apart; they avoided each other's eyes. (166-167)

Zora and Bles allow dominant society to define them, even though dominant society takes an active part in creating the debased reality they then reject and label as unacceptable. Upon Zora's confirmation of her lack of purity, Bles rejects her excuse of ignorance: "All women know! You should have died!" (170). The feeling that action as drastic as suicide must be taken to prevent the corruption of Black womanhood was present in *Blake, Imperium*, and *Of One Blood*. But Du Bois, instead of perpetuating the idea that suicide is a solution for lost chastity, presents a survivor's spirit in Zora's resiliency. In Du Bois's view, in the forming of a domestic Black nation,[10] there must be acknowledgement of the oppression in the history of the community (slavery, rape, destruction of the Black home), but also a learning from these experiences upon which to build a foundation for community success. Instead of blaming Black women for the history of rape and sexual oppression, which Bles does, and as Delany, Griggs, and Hopkins implicitly do, Du Bois suggests that the responsibility be placed on the oppressor. Du Bois further suggests that the Black community must then question their acceptance of a white value system as a path to inclusion and recognize the hypocrisy of such a choice.

Bles, in rejecting Zora and leaving the swamp community, because of her unacceptable (to him) sexual history, also rejects the gifts that come from the masses; in leaving Zora, he also leaves the dream of the silver fleece, the dream of Black separation and autonomy. This great loss causes Zora to sink temporarily into despair. Zora adamantly rejects religion to pacify the pain she feels: "I want no prayers! ...I will not pray! He is no God of mine. He isn't fair. He knows and won't tell. He takes advantage of us—he works and fools us" (181); this echoes Delany's sentiments expressed in *Blake*. Zora sees no use in religion for her as a Black woman, but rather sees the Christian God as working for her oppressors. Although she is distraught at the loss of Bles, Zora's commitment to the fleece remains strong and she pours her energy into the harvesting of the crop. Bles's abandonment of Zora, representative of the Talented Tenth abandoning the masses, leaves the latter (Zora/the folk) once again vulnerable to white supremacy.

Zora, less educated but left with the gifts of blackness (the silver fleece and double consciousness), is once again left unprotected and is again "raped"—financially this time—by the Cresswells; they steal the special cotton crop—the silver fleece. According to Bles's rules, rape should equal death and therefore the rape of the silver fleece should "kill" Zora. But just as she survives her own rape, the rape of the fleece also stirs in Zora a survival instinct. Moreover, having already survived her own rape, Zora is empowered:

> [H]er hand closed almost caressingly on a rusty poker lying on the stove nearby; and as she sensed the hot breath of him [Harry Cresswell] she felt herself purring

in a half heard whisper. 'I should not like—to kill you.'
(187)

Because of Zora's love of blackness (in herself and in the community), the oppression she experiences does not turn her to inward violence, but outward. Moreover, Du Bois writes that oppression—racial, sexual, and economic—is the cause of the veil being forced upon the Black community:

> Somewhere in the world sat a great dim Injustice which had veiled the light before her young eyes, just as she raised them to the morning. With the veiling, death had come into her heart. (188)

What becomes dead for Zora, in the face of racial injustice, is the dream of inclusion brought to life through the strategy of racial uplift. Yet, because of her connection to the Black community, her resolve to succeed is strengthened through a separatist plan. By contrast, Bles, when faced with injustice, and with the Cresswells stealing Zora's chastity, becomes blind to Zora's value, and thereby the value in blackness/the folk, but becomes more resolved to seek inclusion in larger society despite his race.

Bles's abandonment of Zora initiates the death of her quest for inclusion, which she began only to please him. Without his presence, Zora begins to work towards a separatist goal. Zora submits to "finish school" with Mrs. Vanderpool in Washington D.C., not for any personal goal, but as a means of reconnecting with Bles. She, moreso than he, recognizes their strength as a union, rather than as individuals—the Talented Tenth in cooperation with the masses. Such motives transform Zora into "Miss Zora," a title of respect given to her by the other members of the swamp community, suggesting a recognition of her superior status, which comes about through education, but also through her commitment to them.

In her return to the swamp, Zora, because of her experiences and opportunities in dominant society, sees her home and her community in a much different way: "She saw hundreds and thousands of black men and women:

crushed, half-spirited, and blind" (355). In Zora's eyes, the swamp community no longer contains dreams and laughter. Her formal education, as well as the temporary access to inclusion she experienced in Washington, D.C. with Mrs. Vanderpool, leaves her with a greater understanding of racial exclusion and oppression. Zora returns with an understanding of dominant society, politics, and business that the swamp community does not have. But more importantly, her homecoming includes a political and economic plan. She explains to Miss Smith that, "We must have land—our own farm with our own tenants—to be the beginning of a free community" (362). Although both Zora and Bles submit to racial uplift, Zora returns to use what she has learned and applies it to a separatist strategy for Black nationhood. On the other hand, Bles's experience with racial uplift creates in him a desire for inclusion within dominant society; hence his move to Washington D.C. and his attempts at a political career. Although he does not completely abandon the masses, as Caroline does, he seeks to reform the whole nation from within, believing essentially in the possibilities of a pure American democracy. It is only after he understands how corrupt the American political system actually is, and experiences the willingness of other "Talented Tenth" African Americans to participate in a corrupt system as a means of progressing, that he abandons the idea of reform from within and returns to the swamp. One might say that Zora's action to buy the swamp, as opposed to taking the swamp by some means, is still a strategy of working from within the system. Such an interpretation essentially is true. But Zora's ultimate goal for the swamp is one of independence from white control and influence—economic and political. Any imagined Black nation on domestic soil must in some way remain connected to the larger nation, usually by economics. Even with Black owned businesses, banks, and government, there is still the same monetary system. In *Quest*, plans for financial independence are still dependent upon the selling of crops within a white American business system. Any imaginings of a domestic Black nation, whether separatist (those of Zora and Bernard) or reformed and inclusive (those of Bles and Belton) include a fundamental belief in the viability of democracy and capitalism.

Even though Zora's commitment to the community and her preparedness for leadership are supported by Miss Smith and Mrs. Vanderpool, and the reader as well, Zora's fitness for leadership is questioned by the community because of what is perceived as her lack of an acceptable religion and her connection to Elspeth, a connection to voodoo. Although the community respects her, she is not fully trusted because of her disconnection from church. Zora encourages the community to think for themselves and to be active participants in their own success: "My own people, I am not asking you to help others; I am pleading with you to help yourselves. Rescue your own flesh and blood—free yourselves—free yourselves!" (370). Although her movement toward action and towards work for the community is motivated by her own spiritual experience, the sermon she heard in Washington D.C., here she suggests that the future success of their work will come solely out of their own labor and not out of any divine providence. Not surprisingly, then, her plan is rejected at first by the spiritual leaders of the community because, "they has to 'low that you didn't say much 'bout religion when you talked. You ain't been near Big Meeting—and—and—you ain't saved" (371). Du Bois echoes the trope found also in the previous novels in this study—the need for a spiritual foundation in the forming of the Black nation and the responsibility of the Black leader to transform a traditional spirituality (seen as oppressive and appeasing) to one more suited for political progress, a liberation theology. The characters of Blake, Belton, and Reuel have all met such a responsibility while at the same time the authors have critiqued the community's need for religion.

Bles returns to the swamp at the height of Zora's reconstruction plans, but unlike her, he returns without any clear-cut ideas about what to do or why he is there. Also unlike Zora, he is not drastically changed in mentality nor outlook. Her own transformation comes as a shock to him and is met with his usual condescension:

> Zora ...was to him a new creature. ....Just what he had expected was hard to say; but he had left her on her knees in the dirt with outstretched hands, and somehow he had expected to return to some corresponding mental attitude. (378)

This reveals Bles's superior attitude (that of the Talented Tenth) to Zora (the New Negro, the folk) even after racial uplift. Even though his dedication to the people, seen through his final statement to Caroline, suggests his valuing blackness, his return to the swamp is also a return to the original triangle/conflict. Just as he must change his opinion and judgement of Zora, he must also break from his valuing of white societal values over Black, symbolized in his relationship with Mary.

His separation (physical, emotional, and psychological) from the masses of the Black community means that his survival skills for living in a hostile environment are not fully developed; his program of racial uplift, designed by white society, does not include the learning of one's vulnerability in dominant society. Thus, here Du Bois stresses Bles's dependence on Zora—the elite's dependence on the masses for their indestructible spirit of survival. Bles's dependence on Mary's advice, symbolic of the Black community's dependence on white America, despite its hypocrisy, continues to place his own success, and ultimately his life, in jeopardy when he returns to the swamp.

Ironically, Zora's act of heroism—saving Bles from being caught in a compromising position with Mary—prompts a marriage proposal from Bles, whereas his previous knowledge of her impurity caused him to reject her. But even this reversal of roles (woman as protector, man as sexually vulnerable to white lust) does not elicit a change in Bles's attitude of superiority over Zora; Zora's rejection of the proposal is a statement that their union (as it currently stands) is an unproductive one. Bles has neither rejected his beliefs in white superiority nor accepted and acknowledged any innate value in blackness. Bles's proposal is still fraught with his commitment to a traditional hierarchy; he assumes that he must lead and Zora must follow. He assumes that he and Zora must marry because he is sexually attracted to her. But we as readers, and the Black community in the text, have accepted Zora as the more competent leader and therefore Bles must adjust his thinking before he can build a partnership with Zora, both personally and professionally. Also, Zora's leadership qualities conflict with traditional roles (white values) of women and wives; thus a marriage to Zora would mean a rejection of these roles and thereby of white values.

Gender Partnership and Domestic Nation Building

In making Zora, a Black (brown skinned) woman the center of the novel, and by the end, the leader of the domestic Black nation (represented as the swamp community), Du Bois presents Zora as "the person of greatest courage, of greatest insight and dignity and power" (Aptheker 119) in the novel. He drastically breaks from the other writers in this study by answering the calls of Delany, Griggs, and Hopkins for Black male and female partnership with his image of Black female leadership. The plot of revolutionary change in the previous novels examined in this study was catapulted into action through the vulnerability of the Black woman: Blake sees futility in attempting to make a life in the States once his wife Maggie is sold; Belton commits to community progress and success when Antoinette gives birth to a "white" child, Bernard becomes a promoter of separatism when Viola commits suicide, and Reuel abandons the quest for inclusion when he believes Dianthe is dead. Even though Black women are the catalysts for revolutionary action in each case, they do not play a prominent role in the planning of the Black nation. In *Blake*, women are tolerated in the meetings but not taken seriously. In *Imperium*, women take no part in the secret organization. Hopkins begins the move away from dominant male leadership, but presents the possibility of Black women as leaders only outside of the States. Although Reuel marries Queen Candace in what appears to be a joint reign over Telassar, Candace is not given an active role. Du Bois begins a serious examination of the importance of Black women as leaders, through the presentation of Zora.

Both Griggs and Hopkins present double consciousness as a burden, one that Belton Piedmont, in *Imperium*, attempts to overcome through his acceptance of a patriotic Christianity and one that Reuel Briggs, in *Of One Blood*, is tortured by. In contrast, Du Bois, in *Quest*, presents this trope as "a gift of second sight," focusing on the positive aspect of double consciousness as presented in his essay[11] through the character of Zora. This gift, not available to Bles, allows Zora to distinguish the racial barriers set up by white supremacy, acknowledge the hypocrisy and myth of white superiority, and recognize situations of racial danger and Black vulnerability. Zora is attributed this gift by Du Bois because she is representative of the excluded section of the African American community; living in the swamp, not formally educated, illiterate, connected to the land, naked, and wild, Zora is that part of blackness which is embarrassing to assimilationists. Yet in *Quest*, Du Bois makes use of this character, and her characteristics, as a means for unifying the community and developing Black success through racial separation. Although Zora, and not Bles, emerges as community leader by the end of the novel, Zora does not lead in her "natural" state; she must first undergo the process of formal education. But unlike Bles, who from the beginning of the novel fully accepts the promises of racial uplift and formal education—and thereby racial assimilation—Zora only endures and submits to the transforming process for the sake of love, indicative of the African American's overwhelming love of his/her native land. She never loses sight of her "home" (the swamp) and her blackness. She also recognizes those "faults" and "defects" in her and her community—those which cause Bles to reject her—as superimposed from the dominant culture and not essentially Black. Because of this, Zora is able to express her anger against the dominant and oppressing society as well as to recognize the vulnerable situation racial integration has placed African Americans in, none of which Bles is able to do. Yet also unlike Delany and Griggs, Du Bois is able to imagine a productive domestic Black nation without revolutionary violence. The positive outlook that this novel offers of possibilities in the birthland for nation and homeplace building is perhaps indicative of Du Bois's own experiences with partial inclusion. But as the political climate grew once again increasingly hostile to blackness, between 1911 and 1928 even Du Bois gave up hope in a domestic nation.

Imagining Global Racial Unity: W.E.B. Du Bois Rethinks Talented Tenth in *Dark Princess*

No race can prosper until it learns that there is as much dignity in tilling a field as in writing a poem.

—Booker T. Washington

The cost of liberty is less than the price of repression.

—W.E.B. Du Bois

It is during the period of the 1920s that the African American community once again considered emigration to some other locale in search of a homeplace, and that the Black nation novel reemerged with a global variation. Keeping with the template set by Martin Delany, W.E.B. Du Bois, after exploring a domestic solution to racial exclusion with his first novel, seventeen years later returned to fiction in order to imagine a global solution. Du Bois moves towards Pan-Africanism and imagining a global Black nation in *Dark Princess* (1928).[1] Unlike Delany and Pauline Hopkins, Du Bois extends the idea of the global nation to include Pan-Africa and Pan-Asia. Also unlike the previous novels in this study, Du Bois once again utilizes the romance genre. The primary ideological task of the romance genre is to assist in the consolidation of an imagined national community; this is accomplished, or attempted, by projecting a harmonious narrative conclusion on a range of disruptive social divisions.[2] In this chapter I will examine the use of the romance as a political tactic for imagining the Black nation which allows the resolution of several issues—the role of Black women in nation formation, the quest for inclusion, and spirituality—that are left unresolved in the previous texts of this study.[3]

Most literary critics view W.E.B. Du Bois's second attempt at a novel as having even less literary merit than his first novel, *Quest*. The bulk of the criticism acknowledges Du Bois's treatment of issues first explored in *Quest*, such as socialism and double consciousness. Du Bois's first two novels differ, though, in his willingness in the second novel to express Black sensuality and sexuality in positive terms, and to do so not only outside the confines of marriage, but through an adulterous liaison. Claudia Tate, in her introduction, concludes that contemporary critics "regarded his erotic effusion as tasteless, inappropriate, even immoral" (xxiii). Tate further concludes in *Psychoanalysis and Black Novels*, that the novel shows Du Bois's "tendency to eroticize racial justice in his writings" (51).

Political readings of *Dark Princess* usually connect the secret council he portrays there with Du Bois's work establishing a Pan-African Congress and his understanding of white supremacy as more pervasive than just Black oppression in the United States. Marion Berghahn, in *Images of Africa in Black American Literature* (1977), sees the novel as "lend[ing] a wider significance to African culture and fus[ing] it with Asiatic culture in order to build up, with the help of this culture of all 'darker peoples' a black counterworld" (108). Richard Kostelanetz, in *Politics in the African American Novel* (1991), sees that, "in *Dark Princess*, not only the South, but also the North is rejected as the novel's protagonist expatriates to India; and the novel predicts that all colored people will claim as their own land they now occupy" (66). Bernard Bell, in *The Afro-American Novel and Its Tradition* (1987), sees *Dark Princess*, as "a chronicle of despair in which the only hope for the world is the rise of an independent, industrialized Africa and Asia under the same banner of socialism and the leadership of Talented Tenth of nonwhite nations" (82). These critics concentrate only on parts one and four of the novel, that is, on Matthew and Kautilya's first meeting and on their reunion; these sections cover Matthew's introduction to the secret council and, at the end, his commitment to a global revolution.

Analysis of parts two and three of *Dark Princess* include a critique of Du Bois's limitations as a fiction writer. Wilson Jeremiah Moses, in *Black Messiahs and Uncle Toms* (1982), although acknowledging Du Bois's use of a messianic character, the child of Matthew and Kautilya, concludes that *Dark Princess* "is certainly more important as a handbook of Du Bois's imagery than as a landmark of Afro-American literature" (154). Eric Sundquist, in *To Wake the Nations* (1993), sees *Dark Princess* as a "split between a sturdy realistic plot and a framing allegory given over to the birth of the Pan-African messiah that is only marginally interwoven into the political drama" (619).

Once again, Arnold Rampersad, in *The Art and Imagination of W.E.B. Du Bois* (1990), has to date given the most serious examination of Du Bois as a fiction writer. He sees in *Dark Princess* an examination of Talented Tenth leadership without much detail or concern for the masses. For Rampersad, the novel's importance lies in Du Bois's extension of the tradition of Black male heroism, begun in "Of the Coming of John," continued in *Quest* with the character of Bles, and brought to fruition with Matthew in *Dark Princess*. He concludes that Du Bois's main characters "all display a vagueness and hesitation in dealing with the world, a susceptibility in manipulation because of this lack of confidence, and in the case of Bles and Matthew, a powerlessness in the face of the ill–chosen Black women preying on their idealism and indecisiveness" (206). Moreover, Rampersad asserts that the "Du Bois black hero has the mark of saintliness in him, a nostalgia for asceticism, a yearning for Puritan self-control, against which the passionate black body steadily rebels" (207).

My examination of *Dark Princess* differs from these critics in seeing the novel primarily as Du Bois rethinking Talented Tenth leadership, an extension of the exploration begun in *Quest*. In both novels Du Bois presents the Talented Tenth as in need of grassroots experience, as well as formal education, in order to become fit for leadership. I find *Dark Princess* crucial to this study of the Black nation novel because, as a response to several calls—calls for a global perspective, for gender inclusion, and for spiritual underpinnings—Du Bois is able to imagine, in a more complete form, what previous writers could not. Kautilya is an extension of Du Bois's belief in Black female capability for leadership. Unlike Zora, Kautilya guides Matthew into grassroots experience, impressing on him the importance of connecting with the masses. Moreover, Kautilya also leads Matthew back to a connection with an African spirituality, represented through his mother, and joined with an Asiatic spirituality, rejecting Christianity. I believe that Du Bois is able to imagine Black female leadership as a vital part of Black nation building primarily because he foregoes a domestic solution and embraces a global revolution. As I have demonstrated in chapters one and three, when authors depart from an emphasis on domestic inclusion, Black female characters are allowed more autonomy and political awareness and importance. Finally, although Moses finds Du Bois's use of a messianic theme formulaic, in my study, the birth of the messianic child is further evidence of Du Bois's ability to completely imagine what previous authors could not. The children in previous texts of this study are not seen as possible messiahs. In Delany's

Blake, Blake's son is unfit for the messianic role because he is born in slavery. Belton's son, in Griggs's *Imperium*, is also unfit due to his "whiteness" at birth. In Hopkins's *Of One Blood* and Du Bois's *Quest*, the couples that are fit for leadership do not consummate their relationships within the novels. But in *Dark Princess*, Du Bois presents Matthew and Kautilya conceiving the hope for a changed future.

Understanding Global Black Connections in Nation Building

Du Bois begins *Dark Princess* with the character of Matthew Towns aboard a ship, leaving America for Europe. His self-imposed exile is a hasty one and not very well thought out. It comes from being expelled from medical school because of his race, after completing two years of study, at the honors level. Matthew's surprise at being expelled suggests that he had been naively confident in racial uplift as a viable strategy for African American progress. For Matthew, without racial uplift as the path to inclusion into America, he can see no other way to survive, and more importantly, thrive.

Matthew recognizes that self-exile means removing oneself from America's white supremacy but also from one's homeland and Black community—all signified in his goodbye note to his mother: "I'm through. I cannot and will not stand America longer. I'm off. I'll write again soon. Don't worry. I'm well. I love you" (5). Although he likes the racial acceptance in Europe, the lack of a homeland and a Black community makes Matthew's experience in Europe a lonesome one. It is in the middle of his homesick musing that Matthew first meets Princess Kautilya at a café, and upon seeing her, he thinks:

> First and above all came that sense of color: ...suddenly, a glow of golden brown skin. It was darker than sunlight and gold; it was lighter and livelier than brown. It was a living, glowing crimson, veiled beneath brown flesh. It called for no light and suffered no

shadow, but glowed softly of its own inner radiance. (8)

Matthew's first impression of the Princess is very similar to Bles's first impression of Zora. Both men see in these women that which they most long for: Bles an African and spiritual connection, and Matthew the embodiment of colored elite, the status from which he was rejected by Columbia. Moreover, he sees in the Princess "no shadow"[4] of inferiority. While Matthew suffers from feelings of inadequacy, due to his experiences of oppression, he views in Kautilya a woman full of confidence.

Although Kautilya is not of African descent, her color is interpreted as Black by the white American males in the café, thus allowing Du Bois to suggest both the need for union amongst people of color and the overarching oppression of white supremacy. The white American men are portrayed as a threat to Black womanhood; although Kautilya is not African American, as a woman of color she is treated as any Black woman would be treated in the States. The white American men ignore the class status of Kautilya, and she becomes just another Black woman available to and under the threat of white male licentious behavior. As her class gives her no protection, her vulnerability again represents Du Bois's questioning of racial uplift as a viable option against white supremacist behavior.

Here Du Bois introduces the theme of the Black male desire to protect Black womanhood, present in all of the texts in this study. The difference in this case is that Matthew succeeds (although he is only able to do so outside his native land) while in the previous texts, the attempt to protect has been futile. The threat Matthew sees approaching Kautilya sparks in him the desire for action, Kautilya is grateful for his protection and repays him with a ride in her car. When Matthew relates for Kautilya, and for the reader, his history of oppression and his attempts at uplift, Du Bois portrays him as representative of the African American community: "It was evidently not of him, the hero, of whom she was thinking, but of him, the group, the fact, the whole drama"

(15). Kautilya has little knowledge of African Americans and the history he recounts informs her in a new way. She responds: "I do not quite understand. But at any rate I see that you American Negroes are not a mere amorphous handful. You are a nation!" (16). Such a statement places Du Bois's novel in dialogue with both Delany and Griggs and the viewing of the African American community as a nation within a nation as discussed in chapters one and two.

A new understanding of the African American community encourages the Princess to bring Matthew into her political confidence. Because Matthew shows courage and willingness to protect Black womanhood, his actions convince Kautilya that African Americans are a people willing to participate in the claiming of the political freedom and autonomy; she explains:

> we are—a part of a great committee of the darker peoples; of those who suffer under the arrogance and tyranny of the white world. . . . We have among us spokesmen of nearly all these groups—of them and for them—except American Negroes. Some of us think these former slaves unready for cooperation. (16)

Du Bois's introduction of the secret movement of which Kautilya is a vital part is historically significant in two ways. First, it departs from the earlier novels in this study by decentering the African American as messiah for global and racial revolution such as was presented by Delany and Hopkins. Secondly, Du Bois here is questioning his own ideas of Pan-African and Pan-Asian unity, proposed first in the Niagara Movement, and the viability of unity across class lines, as first presented by Delany in *Blake*. The stereotype of the African American as passive, presented by Du Bois as a global idea through Kautilya's comment about African Americans, is challenged by Matthew's action in her defense. It is this action, or confidence in action, which gives him access into the revolutionary society and offers for the Princess the possibility of a reinterpretation of her assumption. She explains her surprise and pleasure at his display of heroism:

> It had never happened before that a stranger of my own color should offer me protection in Europe. I had a curious sense of some great inner meaning to your act—some world movement. (17)

Kautilya's confidence in the significance of Matthew's action propels him out of a state of inferiority and self pity: "For the first time since he had left New York, he felt himself a man, one of those who could help build a world and guide it" (18).

Matthew's introduction to the "Princess and the Council of the Darker Races" offers for him a new avenue of power and progress—"Here was power, and here he had some recognized part. God! If he could just do his part, any part!" (24)—but the role available to him is partly limited by his race and by the Council members' perception that African Americans lack initiative. Matthew undergoes a mental transformation after his encounter with the "Princess and the Council," one in which he realizes he has a responsibility to the pursuit of Black success beyond his own personal achievement. In contrast to his earlier fleeing of the States without a purpose when he was rebuffed, now he uses the new slight as a motive to return to the States energized for change:

> He wanted to get his hands into the tangles of this world. He wanted to understand. His revolt against medicine became suddenly more than resentment at an unforgivable insult—it became ingrained distaste for the whole narrow career, the slavery of mind and body, the ethical chicanery. His sudden love for a woman far above his station was more than romance—it was a longing for action, breadth, helpfulness, great constructive deeds. (42)

Matthew's introduction to a colored global power initiates his return to the States. Here Du Bois veers from the template established by Delany, and extended by Hopkins, of giving up on the domestic situation and moving towards a global solution. Unlike Delany and Hopkins, Du Bois, in his second novel, moves from the global to the domestic and then back to the global, because he wants the American domestic scene to profit from the new global achievement.

Rethinking Domestic Nation Building

Part two of *Dark Princess* addresses Matthew's return to the States and his attempt to find brave and serious revolutionaries who would prove the value of the African American community to the Council. Du Bois uses this section of the novel to explore the racial lines which prevent class consciousness and unification against capitalism and monopoly, and class lines that are drawn within the Black community which prevent a united front against white supremacy. Matthew's return to the States is also a return, mentally and physically, to his mother—who represents his African and folk roots. While in Europe with the Council, Matthew's viewpoint concerning his African roots is mostly a recognition of oppression:

> We American blacks are a very common people. My grandfather was a whipped and driven slave; my father was never really free and died in jail. My mother plows and washes for a living. We come out of the depths—the blood and mud of battle. (23)

But on his return Matthew thinks about his mother—and thus Black people generally—more as survivors: "He could see again that mother of his—that poor but mighty, purposeful mother—tall, big, and brown. What hands she had—gnarled and knotted; what great, broad feet. How she worked!" (37). Here Matthew begins to see value in manual labor, that which represents the work of the majority of the community.

In his search for revolutionary comrades, Matthew comes across Perigua, a revolutionary but awkward thinker. Perigua's boldness, as well as his desire for and commitment to notoriety come in sharp contrast to Matthew's experience with the low key and secret Council.

Moreover, pursuing revolutionary ideals, Perigua stands in contrast also to the visions in the other texts in this study, in which the authors have expressed the desire and need for secrecy in planning a successful Black nation and/or developing the necessary strategies for battling white supremacy. Although Perigua is presented as a lover of pomp and circumstance, his concerns are not altogether flimsy. His office contains a large flag of the United States marked with clusters of little Black flags representing lynchings and riots of the last ten years. His plans for putting a stop to this racial violence include "Dynamite for every lynch mob. . . . There's a lynching belt. We'll blow it to hell with dynamite from airplanes. And then when the Ku Klux Klan meets some time, we'll blow them up. Terrorism, revenge, is our program" (46). Although such a strategy seems drastic and makes Matthew uncomfortable, it is an option that is considered in both reality and fiction.[5] Perigua is convinced that such a plan is one that would find support among the masses but not among the "talented tenth": "the real Negroes—the masses, when they know and understand, most of them are too ignorant and lazy—but when they know! Of course, the nabobs and aristocrats, the college fools and exploiters—they are like the whites" (47). Du Bois's presentation of the radical leader Perigua, as a violent revolutionary, works in direct contrast to Delany's portrayal of Blake, an Afro-Cuban. Whereas Blake is "the recipient of Delany's admiration; Perigua is the butt of Du Bois's contempt . . . [Blake's] make-up is predicated upon self-love; Perigua's upon self-hate" (Rahming 20). But if we examine the role of Perigua in the novel, and as the novel fits in this study of imagining the Black nation, Perigua's revolutionary plans help to reveal Matthew's own inner conflict. Through Perigua, Du Bois deepens his lifelong examination of the Talented Tenth versus the New Negro and the strategies each employs for Black survival and success.

In part one of *Dark Princess*, Matthew is defined for

the reader as a member of the Talented Tenth by virtue of his ability to attend Columbia University medical school and his expatriation to Europe once he is expelled. In North America he is considered to be of the elite Black community. This status is confirmed by the reprimand he is given for working as a Pullman Porter in part two, by a Black woman who recognizes that he is an educated man. Yet among the members of the Council, he is considered as belonging to the lowly by virtue of his race and his heritage of enslavement. Although he comes from the folk, his grandfather having been a slave and his parents sharecroppers, he is disconnected from the experience of manual labor. He is also disconnected from the laboring community as we see in the ease with which he is able to leave his mother after experiencing racial prejudice and denied opportunity.

Perigua, on the other hand, is in the midst of the folk, living and working in Harlem, knowledgeable about where to receive information, and aware of the atrocities committed against Black people nationally (his Black flags signifying lynchings). He is known by the Black working community and has even infiltrated the enemy's camp (the Ku Klux Klan) in order to keep abreast of racist conspiracies. Unlike Matthew, Perigua has faith in the working masses but none in the elite, as the latter are, in his view, too comfortable with their own individual progress. Perigua, not uneducated but also not refined, therefore belongs in the category of New Negro. Also, because of his interest in immediate physical action against oppression (blowing up the towns that allow lynchings, blowing up the train carrying the Klan, aggressively seeking money) Perigua challenges the ideal of working within the system as well as the value of the system (democracy).

Another examination by Rahming suggests that Perigua "is the catalyst of the temporary downfall of the protagonist or, seen another way, he is the chief obstacle to [Matthew's] promising work with a nationalist organization of the darker races of the world" (Rahming 18). While Matthew is usually presented as controlled and educated, and Perigua as emotional and blood-thirsty, by the end of part two, the reader notices Matthew's impulsive nature when he is in a position of disempowerment, especially when he is shocked by exclusion. He first boards a ship for Europe when expelled from medical school without much money or a plan. He initiates a physical altercation with white men in a café over a woman he does not know. He returns to the States prompted by an international political organization that excludes him, once again without money or a plan. He then decides to "join" Perigua in violent action because his leadership in organizing a strike against the railroad fails.

Matthew initially rejects Perigua's plan of action, as well as any confidence in self-determination for the masses. Although Matthew recognizes Perigua's intelligence, he feels disconnected from the motivation of the revolutionary action, which he defines as anger and poverty, neither of which Matthew experiences personally. His own exclusion from dominant society does not produce anger but disappointment, confusion and genuine surprise. He does not experience real poverty as we never see him hungry, homeless or destitute; he works as a Pullman porter in part two but he is still able to dress well and entertain himself.[6]

Matthew's rejection of Perigua as a leader is founded in his commitment to reform from within. The fact that he sees the Black community, with which he is willing to recognize and align, as intertwined with the dominant society in terms of goals and values, is indicative of his commitment to domestic reform and not revolution. Moreover, Matthew's trust in racial uplift is a belief that that class distinctions can overcome racism—even though he himself has been rejected because of race. Perigua, on the other hand, represents a loss of faith in reform from within and a clear understanding of the pervasive oppression based on racial distinctions. He is strongly opposed to passive resistance, finding it ineffective, explaining to

Matthew:

> You've got to yell in this world when you're hurt; yell
> and swear and kick and fight. We're dumb. We dare not
> talk, shout, holler. And why don't we? We're afraid,
> we're scared; we're congenial idiots and cowards. Don't
> tell me, you fool—I know you and your kind. Your
> caution is cowardice inbred for ten generations; you
> want to talk, talk, talk and argue until somebody in pity
> and contempt gives you what you dare not take. (61)

Perigua argues for action over convincing the dominant
society to understand their faults and accept African
Americans. He has no faith in dominant society to give up
any power, wealth, or opportunities. Perigua and Matthew
represent the two choices for Black success, the two warring
selves Du Bois discusses in *Souls*. The self-destructiveness
of such an inner war is represented in Perigua's demise; his
eagerness for violence causes his own death from a
premature explosion of dynamite. Their temporary alliance
leads Perigua to his death and Matthew to a jail sentence.

An Unsuccessful Attempt at Domestic Inclusion

Part three of *Dark Princess* introduces the character
of Sara Andrews, whom Du Bois wants us to contrast with
Kautilya. As a political player, Sara "had no particular
scruples or conscience. Lying, stealing, bribery, gambling,
prostitution, were facts that she accepted casually" (112).
But personally she is strictly chaste. Although she is highly
successful, through her Du Bois continues his critique of
racial uplift. Sara, educated and willing to work within the
system, has also taken on the negative attributes of corrupt
white society. Aware of the handicap that her race forces
upon her, she acknowledges the stereotypes that dominant
society would have her fill, i.e. that she be sexually
promiscuous, uneducated, crude, and poor, and works hard
against those. While she represents the success of uplift on
an individual level, Sara has little community concern.

Through Sara, Du Bois critiques those African

Americans involved in politics for personal glory instead of community and national change. Also, Sara is presented as the real force behind the political actions of Matthew. Here, the reader may question Du Bois's commitment to female equality and Black female leadership. But it is important to recognize several issues in his presentation of Sara. First, in comparison to Zora and Kautilya, she is more connected to whiteness as a "near-white" mulatta, therefore a union with this woman can be seen as the willingness to value whiteness over blackness; Du Bois presents such unions as counterproductive to Black nation formation and our male protagonists end up with the brown women (Zora and Kautilya) rather than the almost "white" women, suggesting their commitment to coloredness instead of inclusion. Second, Sara is willing to use corrupt means towards individual success. Third, she envisions her own success as dependent upon the status of her husband and is willing to marry for status rather than love. Fourth, she has little concern for the struggles of the community. And last, she is materially oriented. Without the opposing characters of Kautilya and Zora, brown skinned women in leadership that are community oriented, the reader might question Du Bois's harsh portrayals of Sara in power positions. Instead, Du Bois is critiquing the dangers of subscribing to a value system that removes a person from blackness and the community.

Matthew's incipient political career is used for community gains, the original purpose of racial uplift. He returns to Virginia, to his mother, and uses his salary to pay off her sharecropping debt. But as he does this, the elite make no effort like his own to assist in the bettering of the folk, and thus he loses faith in a national movement of freedom and uplift. As we have seen before, Matthew is impulsive in his decisions. It is this "death of faith" that propels Matthew into alliance with Sammy and Sara and corrupt politics for personal gains. He goes so far as to marry Sara, a woman for whom he has very little attraction, because, according to her, "enlightened self-interest calls us to be partners" (138). This marriage takes Matthew away from the interests of the Black community and allows him to forge an allegiance with the white values of materialism and corrupt politics. Moreover, a move away from the community is also a move away from love and nurturing; alliance with whiteness in both these novels puts one in a hostile environment. To Matthew marriage represents a certain respectability that in turn will fill some desire for inclusion that he has also sought through political strategy. By contrast Sara sees marriage as another strategy for fulfilling personal ambition.

Just as a "marriage" of the Black community into dominant society yields no true equality or opportunity—assimilation has only yielded second class citizenship (grandfather clauses, Jim Crow laws, continued lynchings, etc.)—Matthew's marriage to Sara also provides no sharing of opportunities. Sara, by virtue of her being able to pass and her willingness to work within the system has accumulated a substantial amount of wealth and material possessions but she is unwilling to share with Matthew. Moreover, their marriage is not presented as a move towards changing either the separation between the races nor that of the classes intraracially. Sara, at their wedding asks Matthews to, "Be careful of the veil" (144); here Du Bois makes reference to his own trope of the veil of separation in *Souls* and further connects Sara to the dominant society. Just as the wedding veil separates her from an intimate connection with her new husband, race separates the African American community from a union with its birth nation. Sara has no interest in connecting with her husband and is committed to protecting the veil that separates them. Likewise America has no interest in forming a union with African Americans and also protects the veil of race that separates the communities.

Matthew's union with Sara, indicating his desire to commit to a domestic and perhaps individual solution, is

144

not successful in eliminating his interest in global change, as we see in Matthew's continued interest in Kautilya, even as a memory. The strategies of deceit and dishonesty to which Sara has Matthew submit, in order to achieve political success, go against his moral conscience:

> He was paying too much for money—money might cost too much. It might cost ugliness, writhing, dirty discomfort of soul and thought. That's it. He was paying too much for even the little money he got. He must pay less—or get more. (149)

Matthew is at first willing to indulge in corruption if he feels adequately compensated because he sees no other option. He sees no successful grass roots organizing and he feels rejected and forgotten by Kautilya and the global organization. Even when he is prompted by possible global alliances, by the abrupt appearance of one of the Council members in his office, he rejects them because he has no faith in the Black community's desire and willingness to work toward freedom.

Matthew's home life leaves him immediately unfulfilled as his marriage with Sara is neither the business partnership she suggested, nor the loving union he had hoped. Sara's rejection of intimacy with Matthew is akin to national racial exclusion, and is the result of the dominant society's unwillingness to be influenced by blackness. Sara's resistance to being "mauled and disarrayed" by Matthew, her husband, is an indication of her view that Matthew (blackness) is inferior and a danger to her "purity"(153). Sara's reaction can be interpreted as the dominant society's fears of real racial integration. Sara does not wish to be influenced or changed by Matthew, but is interested in retaining her power over his actions and decisions. Matthew, although willing to become corrupt, is not willing to give up his autonomy. Matthew associates money with freedom because he sees Sara in power in their marriage because she owns everything. While financial independence might grant Matthew freedom from his controlling wife, it would do little in dominant society. Sara, even though she is financially stable, is only marginally accepted when she is recognized as a Black woman; Kautilya suffers the same sexual harassment forced upon other recognizably Black women. Moreover, Matthew forgets his own rejection by society at the beginning of the novel. Sara attempts to secure his compliance with her plans by withholding money from him: "I have drawn out all the money in our joint account and put it in my own account. Everything we have got stands in my name, and it is going to stand there until you get into Congress" (191). Her blackmail here parallels the hegemony enforced by the dominant society, allowing monetary rewards for blind following, and using monetary refusal as a punishment for independent thinking. When Matthew ultimately decides that he is willing to act outside of the prescribed box Sara has planned for him, it is a clear indication of his willingness to abandon the ideology of reform and racial uplift.

Sara's desire that Matthew be elected to Congress is the culmination of her labor towards acceptance and inclusion from dominant society, indicative in the dinner party she arranges to secure this result, to which she has invited the wealthiest and most powerful of the white community along with the most elite of the Black community. The success of her dinner would symbolize the possibility (and hopefully the probability) of full Black equality on domestic soil; the reality instead suggests that "no social affair of whites and Negroes could come to any real conclusion" (195). It is at this dinner that Matthew makes his final break with pursuing white acceptance and inclusion by declaring publicly his love for Kautilya before his wife and her guests, thus sabotaging any political aspirations that may have been possible. During their separation, Matthew and Kautilya have taken separate paths; she has moved closer to the oppressed masses, and he has moved further away from them. Hers has been a spiritual quest, but his has included the selling of his soul and morals. Her path has made her more suitable for partnership and leadership, while his has made him unworthy of such a union: "The Princess that I worshipped is become the working woman whom I love. Life has beaten out the gold to this fine stuff. But I, ah, I am unchanged. I am the same flying dust" (209).

Blackness and Pan-African Nation Building

All four sections of the novel are titled according to Matthew's mental progress: part one "The Exile;" part two "The Pullman Porter;" and part three "The Chicago Politician." Part four, "The Maharajah of Bwodpur" signifies Matthew's development into a global leader, but the title also embodies alliances between African Americans and other dark peoples of the world. This last section of the novel catches the reader up on the spiritual and political growth that Kautilya has undergone in her separation from Matthew. A major obstacle that had to be overcome before she could become an effective global leader was her own privilege and caste. Her education must include her coming to understand herself as a person of color, which had been absent in her political consciousness because of her birth as royalty. Although she is charmed by what Europe has to offer—wealth, opportunities, culture, and civilization—she gradually comes to understand that acceptance by and from Europe also means acceptance of white privilege and white supremacy. Kautilya's realization of the insignificance of her class status in the face of white supremacy initiates the growth of her political consciousness: "It seemed that the scales had fallen from my eyes. I understood a hundred incidents, a dozen veiled allusions and little singular happenings" (231). Here Du Bois uses the scales metaphor to allude to the tropes of the veil and double consciousness he discussed in *Souls* to indicate all people of color experience the same duality of perspective in the face of white supremacy and privilege. It is this shared racial experience that must be used as the foundation for alliances that transcend national borders, racial lines, and spiritual differences.

An ultimate marriage between Matthew and Kautilya cannot take place until both parties break ties to white supremacy; for Matthew this is a break from Sara and the search for inclusion into dominant society. The passionate and nurturing bedroom scenes between Matthew and Kautilya indicate the union of people of color as more natural and more productive than the pursuit of assimilation within the white power structure. But Kautilya does not ask or influence Matthew to divorce Sara; instead she suggests that he return to Sara if she will accept the real Matthew. Tell her, Kautilya says, "'See, I am a laborer: I will not lie and cheat and steal, but I will work in any honest way.' If it still happens that she wants you, wants the *real* you ... if she wants this man, I-I must let you go. For she is a woman; she has her rights" (260). Kautilya's argument transcends the simple marriage between Matthew and Sara and applies equally to the marriage between African Americans and America. Du Bois expressed in *Souls* the desire of the African American to be both Negro and American. If America is willing to accept the "real" African American, that is without forcing him/her to undergo a transformation of racial uplift in the hopes of inclusion, then a global alliance based on race need not be pursued. But because dominant society remains committed to excluding blackness from the nation, global identity is the logically solution to exclusion and white supremacy. Unlike Kautilya, and the other representatives in the Council, the African American (Matthew) has a different relationship to white supremacy. Asia and Africa are geographically separate from Europe and therefore logically should also be politically separate. "Africa America" remains geographically tied to America (Matthew is legally married to Sara) and must either be willing to make an honest attempt at reconciliation (accepting each other as equals) or decide to split forever (divorce and emigration). Kautilya says of Sara, "for she is a woman; she has her rights" (260), but is also speaking of the American nation. Both Delany and Du Bois claim America as their birth land (both using the term "fatherland" for Africa) and therefore "the woman" is America who has "birthed" this community of African Americans.

Matthew's recognition of the improbability of such reconciliation indicates his acknowledgment of America's commitment to racial exclusion addressed in all of the texts in this study:

> But she will not want me; I grieve to say it in pity, for I suffer with all women. Sara loves no one but herself. ...No, she will not want me. But—if you will—as you have said, hers shall be the choice. She must ask for divorce, not I. And even beyond that I will offer her fully and freely my whole self. (260)

Again if we understand this discussion as pertaining beyond the actual marriage, Matthew acknowledges the nation's commitment to racial exclusion and its inability to value anything other than whiteness. He also expresses the patriotism found (and explored with other texts in this study) in the African American community to their birthland. It is this patriotism which creates the conflict regarding a complete separation. Matthew's insistence on Sara making the decision for divorce is seen as the African American community's continued hope for inclusion until faced with blatant rejection.

Further analysis of Matthew's two marriages comes through an examination of their fruits. While Matthew and Sara's marriage is a loveless union, Matthew and Kautilya's is filled with passion. While Sara is adamantly opposed to having a child, Kautilya gives birth not only to a son, but to a "messiah." The creation of this child signifies success in the union of Africa and Asia, but more importantly, the ultimate success of the global Black nation. In relation to this study, the importance of *Dark Princess*, as a Black nation novel, ending with the birth of a messiah, is indicative of Du Bois's ability to imagine a more complete nation than the authors prior to him. First, we see the presence of a child in only two of the four novels prior to *Dark Princess*: *Blake* and *Imperium in Imperio*. In both cases, the child is born prior to imagining the Black nation. In both cases, the child symbolizes an attempt at a domestic solution. And the marriages from which the children are conceived are not presented as proper foundations for the Black nation. Blake and Maggie have a son, but that child is considered property because his parents are enslaved and are also considered property. Blake must both "steal" his son and purchase his wife before forming the stable family foundation for an imagined Black nation. The instability of this family is the catalyst for his revolutionary thought, not the product of the new Black nation. The situation is similar in *Imperium*. Belton and Antoinette also have a son, but their marriage is no more secure than Blake and Maggie's, even though the birth of their son takes place after the war. Once again it is instability that prompts Belton into revolutionary action and Black nation building. Their son is not presented as a link to the future, but a tie to the past, a past of oppression, hegemony, and a lack of self-determination.

The other two novels in the study, *Of One Blood* and *Quest of the Silver Fleece*, do not present births at all, suggesting the inability of the Black communities of these times to envision fully the future of the imagined nations presented. In *Of One Blood*, the domestic union is presented as barren; Dianthe and Reuel find themselves in a false marriage as brother and sister, but even before they realize this, they are unable to consummate their union due to the destruction of the Black family by white supremacy (Aubrey). The "marriage" of Dianthe and Aubrey (a union of "white" and "Black" America) is presented as oppressive and fatal to Dianthe. This marriage is consummated but through force and coercion, and is further considered an abomination because of their sibling relationship. The final marriage presented in the novel, that of Candace and Reuel, is symbolic of the reunion of Africa and "Africa America" as well as the past and the future. Although this union is hopeful, Hopkins does not imagine the future product resulting from this union.

In *Quest*, Du Bois examines the struggles involved in forming productive unions. Bles and Zora do not rush into marriage but analyze the possible repercussions of such unions on themselves and the community. In *Quest*, Du Bois explores the importance of proper preparation prior to marriage; he uses the theme of marriage as a strategy for developing the proper foundation of the imagined Black nation. But although the final union of Bles and Zora is presented as the best foundation for community leadership, perhaps because it is a domestic solution, Du Bois is unable to envision the future of this nation and therefore we have no progeny from this marriage. As Du Bois moves to imagining a global Black nation, as in *Dark Princess*, he is able to envision the future as well, represented through the child born to Kautilya and Matthew. Du Bois's insistence on the birth of a male child has twofold significance: first, he believes in the necessity of male leadership: "for had it been a girl child, I must have left both babe and you. Bwodpur needs not a princess but a king" (308); second, there are only two choices—Africa and Asia must unite for global success, or they must be subject to Europe and America: "If I had not borne your son, I must have gone to prostitute my body to a stranger or lose Bwodpur and Sindrabad; India; and all the Darker World" (308). When Matthew is free from Sara—divorced—he is available to Kautilya; and, when "Africa America" separates itself from America, it is available to unite on a global level. In this union a prophesy is set: "In 1952, the Dark World goes free—whether in Peace and fostering friendship with all men, or in Blood and Storm—it is for Them—the Pale masters of today—to say" (297). Out of this prophecy, the child/messiah will complete the task begun by the proper foundation of the marriage/union between Kautilya and Matthew, Asia and Africa.

Several times during their reunion Kautilya hints at Matthew's separation from America and his joining a global community. She states, when explaining her responsibility to her country, "For of me my people have a right to demand one thing: a Maharajah in Bwodpur, and one—of the blood royal!" (261). We have seen Kautilya's dismantling of the caste system through her work in England, India, and America. And her statement to Matthew after he has become a laborer in the truest sense suggests a redefining of the understanding of royal blood. This redefining and acceptance of the African American as a part of the royal blood line descendant from his/her original continent parallels Hopkins's choice of the African American Reuel as direct heir to the throne by way of his lotus birthmark. In both cases, with Du Bois and Hopkins, the African American is directly connected to royalty through the maternal side of his heritage; this suggests the need for the acceptance and acknowledgment of the Black woman in the process of nation building.

Kautilya does more than accept Matthew's mother (although that alone is more than Matthew has done). She also sees value in Mrs. Towns, which is symbolic of valuing a slave past. Mrs. Towns's slave past connects her to a global past, one with which Kautilya is more familiar. Mrs. Towns, as Black mother, is presented as a connection to spirituality. Matthew's early expatriation was also a voluntary separation from his mother. But it is Kautilya who makes clear to Matthew his need for this spiritual connection through her own search for, acceptance of, and finally refuge in Mrs. Towns. First, Kautilya seeks out Matthew's mother as an attempt to remain connected to him during his time of incarceration. What she finds she interprets on a more personal level: "Your mother is Kali,[7] the Black One; wife of Shiva[8], Mother of the World!" (220). Kautilya places Mrs. Towns in the spiritual realm first and foremost. She is transferred into Hindu history/spirituality, recognizing blackness as existing outside of Africa, in Asia as well. Although Kautilya acknowledges the familiar interpretation of blackness as evil or negative, she places this evil alongside a more nurturing image. In defining Mrs. Towns as wife of Shiva, Kautilya suggests that she will be the force that unites what has been divided; through such action, a new world—imagined community/nation—is given birth.

Unlike Matthew who has attempted to remove himself from the heritage he believes to be his mark of inferiority (he leaves the South for the North, he seeks a professional career instead of an agricultural one, and he does not subscribe to any religion), Kautilya embraces her heritage and finds it to be uplifting. She also sees geographical borders transcended through the sharing of histories:

> And when I saw that old mother of yours standing in the blue shadows of twilight with flowers, cotton, and corn about her, I knew that I was looking upon one of the ancient prophets of India and that she was to lead me out of the depths in which I found myself and up to the atonement for which I yearned. (221)

The significance of Kautilya's interpretation of her experience in the presence of Mrs. Towns is that she sees herself as inferior, having fallen, although she is the ultimate embodiment of racial uplift. Kautilya also sees Mrs. Towns, traditionally considered as inferior—by both dominant white society and the Black elite—as possessing the power to "uplift" her. Thus, Du Bois extends his critique of racial uplift being dependent upon a connection to and valuing of the masses in order to be successful.

Part of Mrs. Towns's powers of uplift come from leading Kautilya to a return to spirituality, an important foundational piece missing. As seen with Delany, there is a hesitancy among African American leaders of subscribing to spirituality because Christianity was taught to the Black community to legitimize passive behavior. The authors in this study have grappled with the rejection of Christianity as an oppressive religion, but they have also acknowledged the inability to unite a group of people around a purely political issue without a unifying spirituality. Delany turns to freemasonry, retaining a trinity found in Christianity but also returning to a spirituality with origins in African civilization; the main component of an imagined Black nation for Delany is a spirituality which prompts action and not passivity. Griggs, though a minister himself, does not offer any final blueprint for spirituality in the forming of a Black nation. Instead, Griggs examines the conflict in nation building ideologies, including and rejecting a spiritual foundation, namely Christianity. As Griggs does not support a mass emigration, but rather is committed to a domestic solution, he does not examine any spirituality outside of Christianity. Hopkins, although imagining the Black nation outside of North America, transports Christianity onto African soil. But at the same time she presents the hidden African community as highly spiritual and similar to Christianity prior to Reuel's leadership, thus suggesting that the origins of Christianity (especially that of the Holy Trinity) have African roots.

In *Quest*, Du Bois attempts to reconcile the acceptance of a pre-Christian spiritual history, presented through the character of Elspeth, and Christianity, but he falls short. Elspeth is never fully removed from the stereotype of savage,[9] and Christianity, outside of its recommendation of selfless work for others, is never fully adopted by Zora. But in *Dark Princess*, the union of Kautilya and Mrs. Towns overtly rejects Christianity and asks for the return to more ancient spiritualities:

> We prayed to God, hers and mine, and out of her ancient lore she did the sacrifice of flame and blood which was the ceremony of my own great fathers and which came down to her from Shango of Western Africa. (221)

Although Kautilya at first assumes differences in the two spiritual heritages (Asia and Africa), she ultimately sees more similarities. Here she connects Hindu with Yoruba religion[10] and notably says nothing about Christianity.

Matthew must undergo a transformation similar to Kautilya's: a recreation of racial uplift through an experience in labor. Here Du Bois suggests that the experience of the masses is the experience of reality. The lives that Kautilya and Matthew were previously living, those of marginal acceptance and inclusion, were actually an illusion; this has become obvious to both of them through their shocking experiences of exclusion. But perhaps more important than Kautilya's enthusiasm, reinforcing the image of her as a more suitable wife/partner than Sara and confirming her new rejection of elitism and privilege, is her ability to connect labor and political work to the dismantling of the oppression of people of color and spirituality. She reinstates spirituality within the foundation of nation building: "Now the time of work dawns. We must go about our father's business" (256). Moreover the act of labor and political work moves the participants into positions of authority: "Oh, Matthew, Matthew, we are rulers and masters! We start to dig, remaking the world" (256). Whereas prior to Matthew's apparent "fall from grace," he found no real value in his heritage as laborer, here Kautilya is able to redefine power in labor and Matthew is willing to do the work of a laborer—both physically, and symbolically as a political revolutionary leader. In addition, Matthew's willingness to labor incites a revolutionary plan:

> We must dig it [our world] out with my shovel and your quick wit. Here in America black folk must help overthrow the rule of the rich by distributing wealth more evenly first among themselves and then in alliance with white labor, to establish democratic control of industry. During the process they must keep step and hold tight hands with the other struggling darker peoples. (256)

Here Matthew, and Du Bois, suggests the connection between

capitalism and racial oppression; thus Black nation building must be a socialist venture. Matthew's plan for African American revolution includes the rejection of assimilation into dominant society, the opposite of what he first pursued.

Du Bois also attempts in *Dark Princess* to present the African American community as operating from a position of power among people of color in the world, quite contrary to the opinion voiced by the Council at the beginning of the novel. First, because of geographical location, "Africa America"—the nation within the nation—is viewed as at the center of America, not as marginal. African Americans, by virtue of living on the same soil, and being a part of the land/nation since its inception, fully belong in the geographical center of their birthland. White supremacy in North America has tried to move African Americans to the margins. Secondly, because of the position of African Americans, the community is endowed with the skill of double consciousness, perhaps missing from other communities of color:

> Singularly enough, we black folk of America are the only ones of the darker world who see white folk and their civilization with level eyes and unquickened pulse. We know them. We were born among them, and while we are dazzled with their deeds, we are seldom drugged into idealizing them beyond their very human deserts. But you of the forest, swamp, and desert, of the wide and struggling lands beyond the Law—when you first behold the glory that is London, Paris, and Rome, I can see how easily you imagine that you have seen heaven; until disillusion comes—and it comes quickly. (233)

The African American community's knowledge of dominant society and its workings may be used to imitate dominant society or used as a powerful tool for revolution. Kautilya, on the other hand, proposes a separate plan for Africa and Asia.

> "In my India, for instance, we must emancipate ourselves from the subtle and paralyzing misleading of England—which divides our forces, bribes our brains,

emphasizes our jealousies, encourages our weaknesses. Then we must learn to rule ourselves politically and to organize our old industry on new modern lines for two objects: our own social uplift and our defense against Europe and America. Otherwise, Europe and America will continue to enslave us," (256-57)

Here Kautilya suggests actual revolution from white supremacist rule and uplift as a means of acquiring self-government and protection from future oppression.

The second separation of Matthew and Kautilya comes because of his need for preparation and his inability to support her. He must complete his transformation, which will prepare him for leadership; this preparation includes his full and voluntary experience as a laborer, his final separation from Sara, and his acceptance of a spirituality. His letters to Kautilya are the working out of philosophical conflicts, which he comes to understand as the obstacles preventing successful union between people of color and revolution. Matthew also begins to open up to the need for and usefulness of spirituality. Yet like Zora in *Quest*, he initially connects labor with God, using language that suggests faith in one's own ability but not in a higher power. While Matthew's preparation is in industrial labor—the digging of a subway tunnel—Kautilya's has been an agricultural experience—as servant and tobacco hand. She also connects with agricultural history, symbolized in Mrs. Towns, a deeper and more positive image of spirituality. Moreover, Kautilya chooses to return to the farm, and Mrs. Towns, as the best place to nurture her seed/crop—Matthew's child—her pregnancy.

In this last section, Kautilya must provide the voice of reason for Matthew. He is vulnerable to pessimism and the view that only overthrow is valuable. He also has not completely found value in blackness and his history, although he has given up elitism and material pursuit. Kautilya must convince him, and remind herself, of the connectedness between people of color—ancient and never-ending. Kautilya recognizes that being on the inside is akin to slavery as it removes the workers from the majority of the community they are working for (this was the reason for Zora's original refusal to board in at Miss Smith's school). Furthermore, the inside position limits one's actions as there is ever the push to desire inclusion. Kautilya ultimately defines the margins, blackness, as being the most productive and most revolutionary site for global nation building.

Kautilya and global organization call to Matthew for a union. His return to the South and to Kautilya begins with a spiritual journey. He now views the child, a product of his union with Kautilya, as a messiah for the future of people of color: "More than wife, Mother of God and my Son! ...This changes the world" (308). The child changes the world through his presence as a positive result of the union between Africa and Asia, but also as the possibility and probability of transforming the differences between the cultures and religions of people of color into a mutually inclusive and productive strategy for self-empowerment.

Completing the Template

Thus in *Dark Princess*, Du Bois is able to completely work out the relationship between the intellectual and the masses, a theme examined in all of the novels of this study but decidedly incomplete in the previous texts. The closest we come to such closure is found in Delany's *Blake*; it is here that the idea of the leader coming out a similar experience of the masses is first formed. Similar in all of the texts is the ideology of leadership having some elite experience, usually that of education that qualifies them for effectiveness. The challenge has been to imagine a leader, apart from the masses in skills and intellect, but not apart from the masses in goals and experience. Du Bois reconciles this issue by redefining the necessary preparation of the leader as a period not of education but of physical labor, allowing a humbling process to take effect.

What Du Bois achieves in *Dark Princess* is a global articulation of Black nations seeking decolonization. This is ultimately a critique of how the imagined global nation was envisioned by Delany and Hopkins, whose move to a global location bordered on perpetuating the colonization of Africa by African Americans. Delany and Hopkins envision the African American as messiah for the now global Black nation, thereby forcing upon Africans and America "civilization" and "spirituality", but accepting little in return. Du Bois, on the other hand, extends the global vision to include Asia as well as Africa (represented by African Americans); each comes to the foundation on an equal level and contributes to the nation building. He chooses to de-center the role of the African American in the global nation from position of messiah, and instead creates a new messiah through the collaborative efforts of both Africa and Asia, symbolized through the birth of Matthew and Kautilya's child.

Although all of these Black nation novels appear in times of domestic crisis, Du Bois is better equipped than the other authors to envision the imagined Black nation in a complete form because of the economic and political gains discerned over the course of history, starting in the antebellum period. By 1928, with the publication of *Dark Princess*, the domestic nation was still racially segregated and exclusive of people of color, Du Bois recognizes the progress in education, in financial independence (to a certain extent), and in political power in the Black community. He chooses to reserve that power, along with a sense of self-determination and autonomy, for the promoting of community success independent of American success but dependent upon the success of global peoples of color. The symbolic marriage of Kautilya and Matthew signifies the strengthening of the foundational family through global means and not domestic solutions.

Also, Du Bois is able to fully articulate the conflict

CHAPTER FIVE

examined throughout all of these Black nation novels regarding the purpose of and usefulness of a spiritual foundation. While retaining the critique of Christianity, as promoted by white America, first introduced with Delany, Du Bois also chooses to redefine both the function of spirituality, as well as to incorporate a spirituality more ancient than Christianity and perhaps more pertinent to the African American situation. Unlike the previous authors, Du Bois is able to find common ground with ancient spiritualities (African and Asian) and present them as nurturing as well as action oriented. Du Bois does not force one religion onto the new imagined community, as both Delany and Hopkins do, but instead merges spiritualities through the focus and acceptance of similarities instead of differences.

And last, Du Bois's choice of the romance as the genre for a Black nation novel allows him to imagine potential closure for the most disruptive social divisions. Although Delany, Griggs, and Hopkins all incorporate some aspects of romance in each of the novels discussed in this study—specifically the instability of the family as catalyst for revolutionary action and the stable family as the foundation for nation building. Du Bois's insistence on centering the romance plot, and intimately connecting revolutionary thought and nation building with the romance, facilitates the completion of both the Black nation and the romance, as the two issues are intertwined. Moreover, it also allows Du Bois to fully incorporate the Black female into the nation building process, an issue questioned or suggested by the other authors but not fully imagined.

Although Du Bois's articulations of the imagined Black nation, as responses to the calls of Delany, Griggs, and Hopkins, offer the reader more closure, it must be recognized that these are not the final responses. Because the Black nation novel appears in times of crisis, when the African American community is feeling most isolated, excluded, and under attack, as long as America consists of a significant African American community, the Black nation novel will appear. Furthermore, as issues change on the domestic front, the response must also change, as we have seen in this study.

ENDNOTES

Notes to Introduction

1. Karl Marx's classic definition is discussed in Jospeh Stalin, *Marxism and the National Question* (Moscow, Foreign Language Pub. House, 1954), William Pfaff, *The Wrath of Nation* (New York: Simon and Schuster, 1993), and Hugh Seton-Watson, *Nation and States* (London: Methuen, 1977).

2. Black nationalism, like nationalism, is often difficult to define. Some discussions on black nationalism that I have found helpful include: John Bracey, August Meier, and Elliot Rudwick, eds. *Black Nationalism in America* (Indianapolis: Bobbs-Merril, 1970), Rodney Carlisle, *The Roots of Black Nationalism* (Port Washington, NY: Kennikat Press, 1975), E.U. Essien-Udom, *Black Nationalism* (Chicago: University of Chicago Press, 1962), Bill McAdoo, *Pre-Civil War Black Nationalism* (New York: The David Walker Press, 1983), Wilson Jeremiah Moses, *The Golden Age of Black Nationalism, 1850-1925* (New York: New York University Press, 1988), Wilson Jeremiah Moses, *Classic Black Nationalism* (New York: New York University Press, 1978), Alphonso Pinkney, *Red, Black, and Green* (Cambridge: Cambridge University Press, 1976), and Sterling Stuckey, *Slave Culture* (New York: Oxford University Press, 1987).

3. In Jeremiah 13:23 there is an allusion to race—"Can the Ethiopian change his skin or the leopard his

spots?" And in Song of Solomon 1:5, The Queen of Sheba declares, "I am dark, but lovely."

4. The legend of The Queen of Sheba's visit with King Solomon is related in 1 Kings 10:1-13 and 2 Chronicles 9:1-12.

5. In Acts 8:27, Ethiopia's beginnings as a Christian nation is related through the conversion of a eunuch: "So he arose and went. And behold, a man of Ethiopia, a eunuch of great authority under Candace the queen of the Ethiopians, who had charge of all her treasury and had come to Jerusalem to worship."

6. For a more detailed discussion of the adoption of the Exodus story and the Psalms verse to African American outlook on their own experiences and their responsibility towards Africa, see Albert J. Raboteau, *A Fire in the Bones: Reflections in African-American Religious History.* (Boston: Beacon Press, 1995).

7. For discussions of the construction of whiteness in a U.S. context, and of the centrality of white supremacy as an aspect of U.S. nation building see Theodore Allen, *The Invention of the White Race* (New York: Verso, 1994); Noel Ignatiev, *How the British Became White* (New York: Routledge, 1995); Matthew Frye Jacobson, *Whiteness of a Different Color* (Cambridge: Harvard University Press, 1999); George Lipsitz, *The Possession Investment in Whiteness* (Philadelphia: Temple University Press, 1998); David Roediger, *The Wages of Whiteness* (New York: Verso, 1999), 6-13; Alexander Saxton, *The Rise and Fall of the White Republic* (New York: Verso, 1997), 186; Richard Williams, *Hierarchical Structures and Social Value* (Cambridge: Cambridge University Press, 1990), 85-86.

8. For a discussion of whitening policies in Latin American and Caribbean contexts, see Gilberto Freyre, *The Mansion and the Shanties* (New York:

Grove, 1963), 260-63; Paolo Freire, *Education for Critical Consciousness* (New York: Continuum, 1973), 25-26; and Aline Helg, *Our Rightful Share: The Afro-Cuban Struggle for Equality, 1886-1912* (Chapel Hill: University of North Carolina Press, 1995), 6-7.

9. For discussions of separatist history through the nineteenth and early twentieth centuries, see John Hope Franklin and Albert Moss, Jr., *From Slavery to Freedom: A History of Negro Americans* (New York: Alfred P. Knopf, 1989), 155-57; Nell Irvin Painter, *Exodusters* (New York: Alfred P. Knopf, 1977); and William H. and Jane Pease, *Black Utopia* (Madison: the State Historical Society of Wisconsin, 1963).

10. Richard Yarborough, in "The Depiction of Blacks in the Early Afro-American Novel" (Ph.D. Dissertation, Stanford University, 1980), asserts that "the term manhood comes to stand for the crucial spiritual commodity that one must maintain in the face of oppression in order to avoid losing a sense of self-worth and second, the connection established between manhood and violent resistance" (167). Also Calvin C. Hernton, in *The Sexual Mountain and Black Women Writers* (New York: Doubleday, 1987), claims that "historically, the battle line of the racial struggle in the United States has been drawn exclusively as a struggle between the men of the races. Everything having to do with the race has been defined and counter-defined by the men as a question of whether black people were or were not a race of Men. The central concept and the universal metaphor around which all aspects of the racial situation revolve is 'manhood'" (38). The idea of nation-building connected to black manhood, the home and family as the foundation of the nation and the necessity to protect the black woman within that foundation, is explored in these novels. These authors strive towards refiguring the role of the black woman within

nation formation that does not always mirror the patriarchal society from which the black nation separates. I examine in this study the ways in which authors build upon each of the prior imaginings in responses to call for black female and male partnership.

Notes to Chapter One

1. All quotes following will be taken from *Blake; or, The Huts of America A Novel by Martin R. Delany*. Ed.: Floyd J. Miller. (Boston: Beacon Press, 1970).

2. See Wiliam L. Andrews, "The Novelization of Voice in Early African American Narrative." *PMLA* 105 (January 1990): 23.

3. The views of Delany writing Blake as an antithesis of Uncle Tom's Cabin are disturbing because they place far too much emphasis on the work of an "outsider's" interpretation of the struggles of the African American community during a crucial political and literary period. While it is true, there is no escaping Stowe and "her awesome monolith of a book," as Richard Yarborough has examined in "The Depiction of Blacks in the Early Afro-American Novel." Every African American would-be novelist desirous of using the theme of slavery and white supremacy in their work had to come to terms with Uncle Tom's Cabin.

4. Barbara Welter, in *Dimity Convictions* (Athens: Ohio University Press, 1976) has characterized this nineteenth century phenomenon as "the attributes of True Womanhood, by which a woman judged herself and was judged by her husband, her neighbors, and society, could be divided into four cardinal virtues-piety, purity, submissiveness, and domesticity...With them she was promised happiness and power" (21).

5. Hazel Carby, in *Reconstructing Womanhood* (New York: Oxford University Press, 1987), examines the

workings of True Womanhood and notes that white women were the means by which to consolidate property through marriage and the birthing of heirs and thus "True Womanhood" was successful for complete control of reproductive white women. On the other hand, enslaved African American women gave birth to property, not heirs, as enslaved people inherited their status from their mothers.

6.   Scott Nearing also lists the final stage as decay and disintegration of the empire.

Notes to Chapter Two

1.   Griggs, born in Texas in 1872, ordained a Baptist minister, wrote and published five novels between 1899 and 1908 through Orion Publishing Company, which he founded and operated. His literary career spanned almost thirty years with a move away from fiction and the completion of an autobiography and several books and pamphlets on African Americans and the race problem in America; his non-fiction was released through the Public Welfare League, also founded and operated by himself. During his lifetime, his love of books and his understanding of literature as a political tool manifested into a collection of over two thousand books. Griggs was a minor race leader but a member and active participant in the militant Niagara Movement, begun by W.E.B. Du Bois.

2.   All quotes following will be taken from *Imperium in Imperio* by Sutton E. Griggs (Miami, FL: Mnemosyne Publishing Inc., 1969).

3.   Robert Emmet (1778-1803) was an Irish nationalist leader who inspired the abortive rising of 1803 and is remembered as a romantic hero of Irish lost causes. He called for a rising of 1803, after an explosion exposed one of his secret arms depots. The ill-

planned insurrection ended in confusion, with most of the supporters misinformed or deserting the plan. Emmet marched with a small band against Dublin castle. On the way, he killed the lord chief justice. Realizing the futility of the insurrection, Emmet hid for a month and was finally captured, tried for treason, and hanged.

4.   The question of the role of women in the Black nation is ongoing in this study. Delany initiates seeing the African American woman is vital through the use of her removal as a catalyst for revolutionary action. Moreover, Delany himself argues for the participation of Black women at conferences and in the novel he attempts to imagine Black female characters as a part, although small, in the planning process of the Black nation. Although Griggs continues the trope of the Black woman as catalyst, he is unable to extend, or even reiterate Delany's attempts of imagining limited participation. As I will examine in chapter three of this study, Pauline Hopkins briefly returns the readers of this study to imagining Black women as partners in Black nationhood leadership, but it is not until W.E.B. Du Bois that this image is fully explored.

Notes to Chapter Three

1.   All quotes following will be taken from "Of One Blood; or, The Hidden Self" in *The Magazine Novels of Pauline Hopkins* (New York: Oxford University Press, 1988). 441-621.

2.   Ethiopia did not escape the European rush of imperialism. Its struggles to remain an independent nation in the late nineteenth century served as an inspiration for African American aspirations to self-determination. Alone among the African countries, Ethiopia succeeded in retaining independent sovereignity in the face of European colonialism. The

political significance of Ethiopia to the African American community must be recognized on two levels. First, it was the only country in the Bible referred to specifically and in a positive way. In 981 B.C., Makeda, the Queen of Sheba, visited King Solomon in Judea. It is believed that during her visit, they conceived a child, Menelik I. In 955 B.C., Menelik mounted the Ethiopian throne, beginning the Solomonic reign of emperors. Ethiopian legend also proclaimed that Menelik traveled to Judea to meet his father and returned with the coveted Ark of the Covenant and as a convert to Judaism. In 70 A.D., Queen Candace established Christianity at her capital, Axum, making Ethiopia the first Christian nation. It is important to recognize that Ethiopia was an African country that converted to Christianity from Judaism. This religious history was important to an African American elite class interested in debunking the European assumption of African heathenism used to justify African enslavement. Second, Ethiopia, moreso than Haiti and Liberia, was seen as an example of what an African nation could accomplish when untainted by the history of European or American imperialism.

3.   See Ann Allen Shockley, "Pauline Elizabeth Hopkins: A Biographical Excursion into Obscurity." *Phylon* 33 (1972): 22-26.

4.   Barbara Christian fails to mention Hopkins as significant in her study *Black Women Novelists: The Development of a Tradition, 1892-1976* (Westport, CT: Greenwood Press, 1980). Christian credits Frances Harper alone as the forerunner of twentieth century African American women novelists.

5.   See *The Schomburg Library of Nineteenth-Century Black Women Writers* collection, edited by Henry Louis Gates and published by Oxford University Press.

6. See Hazel Carby, "Introduction." *The Magazine Novels of Pauline Hopkins.* New York: Oxford University Press, 1988.

7. In 1900 she published her first novel, *Contending Forces: A Romance Illustrative of Negro Life North and South,* issued by the Colored Co-operative Publishing Company. In the preface of the novel, Hopkins writes that she wants" to do all she can in a humble way to raise the stigma of degradation from [her] race." Her work with the CAM as fiction writer and editorial columnist sought to do just that. Contending Forces offers a fairly conservative treatment of racial mixture, using the theme as a key source of irony and examining the idea that happiness is tied not simply to the absence of exclusion but to the open, ready inclusion of Blacks in the larger society-the logical conclusion of the assimilationist argument. The novel follows in the sentimental novel tradition, examining the life of Black women, the long-term effects of slavery in the Black family, and the necessity for strong family ties. CAM also serialized three novels by Hopkins during her tenure as literary editor.

8. Walker warned, "Never make an attempt to gain our freedom or natural right, from under our cruel oppressors and murderers, until you see your way clear, when that hour arrives and you move, be not afraid or dismayed; for be you assured that Jesus Christ the king of heaven and earth who is the God of justice and of armies, will surely go before you."

9. For detailed discussion on the differences between Crummell and Blyden, see George M. Frederickson, *Black Liberation* (New York: Oxford University Press, 1995).

Notes to Chapter Four

1.   All quotes are taken from the following edition: W.E.B. Du Bois, *The Souls of Black Folk* 1903. (Boston: Bedford Books, 1997).

2.   All quotes are taken from the following edition: W.E.B. Du Bois, *The Quest of the Silver Fleece* 1911. (Chicago: Northeastern University Press, 1989).

3.   Other novels published during this time period include: F.W. Grant's *Out of Darkness* (1909), which promoted Du Boisian politics; Oscar Michaeux's *Conquest* (1913), a story about a successful Black homesteader; Michaeux's *Forged Note* (1915), a semi-autobiography about the frustrations of a Southern black novelist who relocates to South Dakota; F. Grant Gilmore's *Problem* (1915), another romance that celebrates the African American male's contribution in the Spanish-American War, but also concludes the community must look towards Cuba as a homeland; Otis Shackleford's *Lillian Simmons* (1915), a promotion of Washingtonians economics in Chicago; and Henry Downing's *American Calvarymen* (1917), an interracial romance exploring the social ties between Black America and Liberia, concludes with a despair in the inclusion of African Americans into the nation and the necessity to look to emigration to Liberia. Most often novels published during this time employed stock interracial romance plots as a means of exploring the problem of the color line and its solution.

4.   In *Souls* Du Bois explains: "We the darker ones come even now altogether empty-handed: there are to-day no truer exponents of the pure human spirit of the Declaration of Independence than the American Negroes; there is no true American music but the wild sweet melodies of the Negro slave; the American fairy tales and folk-lore are Indian and African; and,

all in all, we black men seem the sole oasis simple faith and reverence in a dusty desert of dollars and smartness" (14).

5. Langston Hughes, in "The Negro Artist and The Racial Mountain," declares of the New Negro artists: "We younger Negro artists who create now intend to express our individual selves without fear or shame. If white people are pleased we are glad. If they are not, it doesn't matter. We know we are beautiful. And ugly too. The tom-tom cries and the tom-tom laughs. If colored people are pleased we are glad. If they are not, their displeasure doesn't matter either. We build our temples for tomorrow, strong as we know how, and we stand on top of the mountain, free within ourselves"" (1271).

6. After reading *Dark Princess: A Romance*, the reader can connect Elspeth with the image of Kali, "the Black One," that Kautilya names Mrs. Towns. Moreover, Elspeth and Mrs. Towns are two sides of the same coin, the Black mother and the Motherland-Africa.

7. Du Bois presents the veil as such: "Then it dawned upon me with a certain suddenness that I was different from the others; or like, mayhap, in heart and life and longing, but shut out from their world by a vast veil" (*Souls* 8).

8. See Henry Louis Gates, Jr.'s *The Signifying Monkey* (New York: Oxford University Press, 1988). He defines signifying as "a technique of indirect argument or persuasion" (54). Although Gates does not examine Zora as a signifying character, I believe Du Bois uses her exactly in this manner.

9. Clearly this suggested prescription for Black nation building becomes problematic, as discussed in chapter one with Delany's emigration plans and chapter two with Hopkin's novel, when one examines

the history of imperialism. A critique of this proposition must include an examination of the potential of African Americans responding to Africa in an imperialist fashion.

10. In 1935, Du Bois published an articled titled "A Negro Nation Within the Nation" *Current History* 42 (June 1935): 265-70, in which he explained, "With the use of their own political power, their power as consumers, and their brain power, added to that chance of personal appeal which proximity and neighborhood always give to human beings, negroes can develop in the United States an economic nation within a nation, able to work through inner cooperation, to found its own institutions, to educate its genius, and at the same time, without mob violence or extremes of race hatred, to keep in helpful touch and cooperate with the masses of the nation" (68). Although written twenty-four years after *Quest*, the ideas proposed by Du Bois in this essay are imagined in detail in the novel. He represents the swamp community and the potential within that Zora develops as the Negro nation he later speaks about.

11. In "Our Spiritual Strivings," Du Bois presents double consciousness as both a gift and a curse:: "...the Negro is a sort of seventh son, born with a veil, and gifted with second-sight in this American world,--a world which yields him no true self consciousness, but only lets him see himself through the revelation of the other world. It is a peculiar sensation, this double consciousness, this sense of always looking at one's self through the eyes of others, of measuring one's soul by the tape of a world that looks on in amused contempt and pity" (8). Although Delany, Griggs, and Hopkins have chosen to focus on the negative aspects of double consciousness, I suggest that the character of Zora is Du Bois's attempt at presenting the positive aspects of double consciousness.

Notes to Chapter Five

1. Kevin Meehan, in examining the Haitian romance, traces a plot development in three Haitian novels that can also be seen to operate in Du Bois's second novel: (1) the male revolutionary nationalist subject appears first as a (heterosexual) romantic hero; (2) although the hero's fate typically entails revolutionary martyrdom, a political legacy endures through the relationship established with a woman in the romantic plot; and (3) erotic potency prefigures historical agency, and the successful "birth" of nationalist consciousness and projects (often allegorized in the literal birth of an heir) depends on a conversion of erotic energies into political energies (107).

2. Doris Summer's observations, in *Foundational Fictions: The National Romance of Latin America* (Berkeley: University of California Press, 1991), about the central connections between the romance genre and nationalism in Latin American cultural history can be applied to Du Bois as well. Three characteristics of the romance that are pertinent to this study include: (1) The romance helps consolidate the nation by articulating its history; (2) Romantic plots typically involve lovers whose desire reaches across social divisions of region, class, race, and religion; (3) The romance examines the close interweaving of erotic and political registers of meaning.

3. The trope of the "shadow: in seem in *Souls*, "I remember well when the shadow swept across me" (7), and in the subtitle of Harper's novel, *Iola Leroy; or, Shadows Uplifted.*

4. Here Du Bois anticipates such literary movements as those expressed in George Schuyler's *Black Empire* and in Toni Morrison's *Song of Solomon* but also

political groups such as the Black Panther Party.

5. In George Schuyler's essay, "Negro Art Hokum," he suggests that middle class African Americans act the same as white Americans of the same status, and suggests similar conclusions for the lower classes of each race, therefore suggesting that nationalism is more influential than race.

6. Kali is presented as a ferocious form of the Goddess in Hindu religion. She is the devourer of time and depicted as having a terrifying appearance, naked or wearing a tiger skin, emaciated, with fang-like teeth and disheveled hair, a lolling tongue, and eyes rolling with intoxication. She is garlanded with human heads, sometimes girdled with severed arms; laughing and howling, she dances, wild and frenzied, in the cremation grounds with a sword and noose or skull upon a staff. She is usually depicted as black. Many Hindus see Kali as representing the realities of death and time; she stands for the frightening, painful side of life which all who desire to progress spirituality must face and overcome.

7. Shiva is a major deity in Hindu religion and the third in the Hindu trinity, along with Brahma and Visnu. Shiva is depicted in the threefold guise of creator, destroyer, and preserver: in this and other images, the faces on either side represent opposites-male and female; terrifying destroyer and active giver of repose-while the third, serene and peaceful, reconciles the two, the Supreme as the One who transcends all contradictions. Shiva is usually depicted with a hand in upright position indicating protection and with a downward pointing hand indicating liberation for all who trust in him.

8. Elspeth, in relation to *Dark Princess*, is certainly represented as the image of Kali, but without an outside (non-North American) interpretation and appreciation of the image of Elspeth/Kali, she

remains unaccepted by the swamp community; she remains misunderstood as a force only of evil.

9. Shango is the Yoruba god of thunder.

Works Cited

Allen, Carol. *Black Women Intellectuals: Strategies of Nation, Family, and Neighborhood in the works of Pauline Hopkins, Jessie Fauset, and Marita Bonner.* New York: Garland Publishers, 1998.

Allen, Theodore. *The Invention of the White Race.* Volume One. New York: Verso, 1994.

— . *The Invention of the White Race.* Volume Two. New York: Verso, 1997.

Ammons, Elizabeth. *Conflicting Stories: American Women Writers at the Turn into the Twentieth Century.* New York: Oxford University Press, 1992.

Anderson, Benedict. *Imagined Communities.* New York: Verso, 1983.

Andrews, William L. "The Novelization of Voice in Early African American Narrative." *PMLA* 105(January 1990): 23-34.

Aptheker, Herbert. *The Literary Legacy of W.E.B. Du Bois.* White Plains, NY: Kraus International Publications, 1989.

— . Introduction. Dark Princess: *A Romance.* Millwood, NY: Kraus-Thomson Organization Limited, 1970.

Athearn, Robert G. In Search of Canaan: *Black Migration to Kansas, 1879-80.* Lawrence: The Regents Press of Kansas, 1978.

Austin, Allan D. "The Significance of Martin Robinson Delany's *Blake; or The Huts of America.*" Ph.D. Dissertation, University of Massachusetts, 1975.

Bakhtin, M.M. *The Dialogic Imagination.* Ed. Michael Holquist. Trans. Caryl Emerson and Michael Holquist. Austin: University of Texas Press, 1981.

Banks, Marva. *"Uncle Tom's Cabin and Antebellum Black Response." Readers in History: Nineteenth Century American Literature and the Contexts of Response.* Ed. James L. Machor. Baltimore: The Johns Hopkins University Press, 1993.

Baym, Nina. *Novels, Readers, and Reviewers: Responses to Fiction in the Antebellum America.* Ithaca: Cornell University Press, 1984.

Bell, Bernard W. *The Afro-American Novel and Its Tradition.* Amherst: University of Massachusetts Press, 1987.

Bell, Howard. Introduction. *Search for a Place: Black Separatism and Africa.* By Robert Campbell and Martin Delany. 1860. Ann Arbor, MI: University of Michigan Press, 1969.

Berghahn, Marion. *Images of Africa in Black American Literature.* Totowa, NJ: Rowman and Littlefield, 1977.

Berzon, Judith R. Neither Black Nor White: *The Mullato Character in American Fiction.* New York: New York University Press, 1978.

Bhabha, Homi K. "DissemiNation: time, narrative, and the margins of the modern time." *The Location of Culture.* New York: Routledge, 1994.

Bone, Robert A. *The Negro Novel in America.* 1958. New Haven: Yale University Press, 1965.

Bracey, John, August Meier and Elliott Rudwick, eds. *Black Nationalism in America.* Indianapolis: Bobbs-Merrill, 1970.

Brodkin, Karen. *How Jews Became White Folk and What That Says About Race in America.* New Jersey: Rutgers University Press, 1999.

Bruce, Jr., Dickson D. Black *American Writing from the Nadir: The Evolution of a Literary Tradition, 1877-1915.* Baton Rouge: Louisiana State University Press, 1989.

Bullock, Penelope L. *The Afro-American Periodical Press, 1838-1909.* Baton Rouge: Louisiana University Press, 1981.

Campbell, Jane. *Mythic Black Fiction: The Transformation of History.* Knoxville: University of Tennessee Press, 1986.

Carby, Hazel V. Introduction. *The Magazine Novels of Pauline Hopkins.* By Pauline Hopkins. New York: Oxford University Press, 1988. xxix-xlviii.

— . *Reconstructing Womanhood: The Emergence of the Afro-American Woman Novelist.* New York: Oxford University Press, 1987.

Carlisle, Rodney. *The Roots of Black Nationalism.* Port Washington, NY: Kennikat Press, 1975.

Carr, Robert. B*lack Nationalism in the New World: Reading the African American and West Indian Experience.* Durham, NC: Duke U.P., 2002.

Christian, Barbara. *Black Women Novelists: The Development of a Tradition, 1892-1976.* Westport, CT: Greenwood, 1980.

Cooper, Anna Julia Haywood. "Womanhood a Vital Element in the Regeneration and Progress of a Race." (1886) *With Pen and Voice: A Critical Anthology of Nineteenth-Century African American Women.* Ed. Shirley Wilson Logan. Carbondale: Southern Illinois University Press, 1995.

Cooper, Frederick. "Elevating the Race: The Social Thought of Black Leaders, 1827-50." *American Quarterly* 24 (Dec 1972):604-25.

Daniel, Walter C. *Black Journals in the United States.* Westport, CT: Greenwood Press, 1982.

Davidson, Cathy N. *Revolution and the Word: The Rise of the Novel in America*. New York: Oxford University Press, 1986.

Delany, Martin R. *Blake; or The Huts of America*. Ed: Floyd J. Miller. Boston: Beacon Press, 1970.

— . *The Condition, Elevation, Emigration, and Destiny of the Colored People of the United States: Politically Considered*. 1852. Baltimore, MD: Black Classic Press, 1993.

— . *The Origins and Objects of Freemasonry: Its Introduction into the United States and Legitimacy Among Colored Men*. Philadelphia: W.S. Haven, 1853.

— . *Principia of Ethnology: The Origin of Races and Color with an Archeaological Compendium of Ethiopian and Egyptian Civilization*. Philadelphia: Harper and Brother Publishers, 1879.

— . "The Political Destiny of the Colored Race." *The Ideological Origins of Black Nationalism*. Ed. Sterling Stuckey. Boston: Beacon Press, 1972.

— . and Robert Campbell. *Search for a Place: Black Separatism and Africa*. (1890) Ann Arbor: University of Michigan Press, 1969.

Doreski, C.K. "Inherited Rhetoric and Authentic History: Pauline Hopkins at the *Colored American Magazine*." *The Unruly Voice: Rediscoverring Pauline Hopkins*. Ed. John Cullen Gruesser. Urbana, IL: University of Chicago Press, 1996.

Douglass, Frederick. "What to the Slave is the Fourth of July?" *The Norton Anthology of African American Literature*. Eds. Henry Louis Gates, Jr. and Nellie Y. McKay. New York: W.W. Norton and Company, 1997.

DuBois, W.E.B. "The Conservation of Races." 1897. *W.E.B. DuBois Reader*. Ed. Andrew G. Paschal. New York: MacMillan Publishing Corporation Inc., 1971.

— . "Criteria of Negro Art." *Crisis* 32 (October 1926). *Within The Circle: An Anthology of African American Literary Criticism for the Harlem Renaissance to the Present.* Ed. Angelyn Mitchell. Durham, NC: Duke University Press, 1994.

——. *Dark Princess: A Romance.* (NY: Harcourt Brace, 1928). Millwood, NY: Kraus-Thomson Organization Limited, 1974.

——. "A Negro Nation Within the Nation." *Current History* 42.3 (June 1953): 265-70. *W.E.B. DuBois Reader.* Ed. Andrew G. Paschal. New York: MacMillan Publishing Corporation Inc., 1971.

——. *The Quest of the Silver Fleece.* (Chicago: McClurg, 1911). Boston: Northeastern University Press, 1989.

——. *The Souls of Black Folk.* (1903). New York: Vintage Books, 1990.

——. "What is Africa to Me?" *W.E.B. Du Bois: A Reader.* Ed. David Levering Lewis. New York: Henry Holt and Company, 1995.

Elder, Arlene. *The Hindered Hand: Cultural Implications of Early African-American Fiction.* Westport, Conn.: Greenwood Press, 1978.

Elliot, R.S. "The Story of Our Magazine." *Colored American Magazine 3* (May 1901):47.

Ernest, John. *Resistance and Reformation in Nineteenth Century African-American Literature.* Jackson: University Press of Mississippi, 1995.

Esedebe, Peter Olisanwuche. *Pan-Africanism: The Idea and Movement, 1776-1963.* Washington, D.C.: Howard University Press, 1982.

Essien-Udom, E.U. *Black Nationalism: Search for an Identity in America.* Chicago: University of Chicago Press, 1962.

——. Introduction. *Resistance and Reformation in Nineteenth Century African American Literature.* Jackson, MS: University of Mississippi Press, 1995.

Franklin, John Hope and Albert Moss, Jr. *From Slavery to Freedom: A History of Negro Americans.* New York: Alfred P. Knopf, 1989.

Freire, Paolo. *Education for Critical Consciousness*. New York: Continuum, 1973.

Frederickson, George M. *The Black Image in the White Mind: The Debate on Afro-American Character and Destiny, 1817-1914*. New York: Harper and Row, 1971.

— . *Black Liberation: A Comparative History of Black Ideologies in the United States and South Africa*. New York: Oxford University Press, 1995.

Freyre, Gilberto. *The Mansion and the Shanties*. New York: Grove, 1963.

Gaines, Kevin. "Black Americans' Racial Uplift Ideology as 'Civilizing Mission'." *Cultures of United States Imperialism*. Eds. Amy Kaplan and Donald E. Pease. Durham: Duke University Press, 1993.

— . *Uplifting the Race: Black Leadership, Politics, and Culture in the Twentieth Century*. Chapel Hill: University of North Carolina Press, 1996.

Garnet, Henry Highland. *An Address to the Slaves of the United States of America*. (New York: J.H. Tobitt, 1848). Nashville, Tennessee: James C. Winston Publishing Company, Inc., 1994.

Gayle, Jr., Addison. *The Way of the New World*: The Black Novel in America. Garden City, NY: Anchor Press, 1976.

Gillman, Susan. "Pauline Hopkins and the Occult: African American Revisions of Nineteenth Century Sciences." *American Literary History*. 8.1 (1996): 57-82.

Gilroy, Paul. *The Black Atlantic: Modernity and Double Consciousness*. Cambridge, MA: Harvard University Press, 1993.

Gloster, Hugh. "Sutton E. Griggs: New Negro Novelist." *The Black Novelist*. Ed. Robert Hemengway.

Griffith, Cyril E. *The African Dream: Martin R. Delany and the Emergence of Pan-African Thought*.

University Park: Pennsylvania State University Press, 1975.

Griggs, Sutton E. *Imperium in Imperio.* (Cincinnati: The Editor Publishing Co., 1899). Miami, FL: Mnemosyne Publishing Inc., 1969.

—. *Light on Racial Issues.* Memphis, TN: The National Public Welfare League, 1921.

—. *The Negro's Next Step.* Memphis, TN: The National Public Welfare League, 1923.

—. *Wisdom's Call.* (1911) Miami, FL: First Mnemosyne, 1969.

Gruesser, John. "Pauline Hopkins' *Of One Blood*: Creating an Afrocentric Fantasy for a Black Middle Class Audience." *Modes of the Fantastic: Selected Essays from the Twelfth International Conference on the Fantastic in the Arts.* Ed. Robert A. Lantham and Robert A. Collins. Westport, CT: Greenwood Press, 1991.

Haskett, Norman Dean. "Afro-American Images of Africa: Four Antebellum Black Authors." *Ufahamu: Journal of the African Activist Association.* 3.2 (1972): 29-40.

Hayford, Casely. *Ethiopian Unbound: Studies in Race Emancipation.* London: C.M. Phillips, 1911.

Hazard, Leland, ed. *Empire Revisted.* Homewood, IL: Richard D. Irwin, Inc., 1965.

Hedin, Raymond. "Probable Reader, Possible Stories: The Limits of Nineteenth Century Black Narrative." *Readers in History: Nineteenth Century American Literature and the Contexts of Response.* Ed. James L. Machor. Baltimore: The Johns Hopkins University Press, 1993.

Helg, Aline. Our Rightful Share: *The Afro-Cuban Struggle for Equality*, 1886-1912. Chapel Hill: University of North Carolina Press, 1995.

Hernton, Calvin C. *The Sexual Mountain and Black Women Writers*. New York: Doubleday, 1987.

Herzog, Kristin. *Women, Ethnics, and Exotics: Images of Power in Mid-Nineteenth Century American Fiction*. Knoxville: The University of Tennessee Press, 1983.

hooks, bell. *Black Looks: Race and Representation*. Boston: South End Press, 1992.

— . *Yearning: Race, Gender, and Cultural Politics*. Boston: South End Press, 1990.

Hopkins, Pauline E. *A Primer of Facts Pertaining to the Greatness of the African Race and Its Possibility of Restoration by Its Descendants*. Cambridge, Mass.: P.E. Hopkins and Company, 1905.

— . *Of One Blood*. (*Colored American Magazine* vol 6, nos 1-11 Nov, Dec 1902; Jan - Nov 1903). *The Magazine Novels of Pauline Hopkins*. New York: Oxford University Press, 1988.

Hughes, Langston. "The Negro Artist and The Racial Mountain." *Within The Circle: An Anthology of African American Literary Criticism from the Harlem Renaissance to the Present*. Ed. Angelyn Mitchell. Durham, NC: Duke University Press, 1994.

Ignatiev, Noel. *How the Irish Became White*. New York: Routledge, 1996.

Jacobson, Mathew Frye. *Whiteness of a Different Color: European Immigrants and the Alchemy of Race*. Cambridge: Harvard University Press, 1999.

Johnson, Abby A. and Ronald M. Johnson. *Propaganda and Aesthetics: The Literary Politics of Afro-American Magazines*. Amherst: University of Massachusetts Press, 1979.

Karenga, Ron. "Black Cultural Nationalism." *The Black Aesthetic*. Ed. Addison Gayle, Jr. Garden City, NY: Doubleday, 1971.

Kassanoff, Jennie A. "'Fate Has Linked Us Together': Blood, Gender, and the Politics of Representation in Pauline Hopkins's *Of One Blood.*" *The Unruly Voice: Rediscovering Pauline Hopkins.* Ed. John Cullen Gruesser. Urbana, IL: University of Chicago Press, 1996.

Keller, Edmond J. *Revolutionary Ethiopia: From Empire to People's Republic.* Bloomington: Indiana University Press, 1991.

Kinshasa, Kwando M. *Emigration vs. Assimilation: The Debate in the African American Press, 1827-1861.* Jefferson, NC: McFarland and Company, Inc., 1988.

Kostelanetz, Richard. *Politics in the African-American Novel.* Westport, CT: Greenwood Press, 1991.

Lemelle, Sidney J. and Robin D.G. Kelley. "Imagining Home: Pan-Africanism Revisited." *Imagining Home: Class, Culture and Nationalism in the African Diaspora.* London: Verso Press, 1994.

Lester, Julius, ed. *The Seventh Son: The Thought and Writings of W.E.B. Du Bois.* Volumes 1 and 2. New York: Random House, 1971.

Levine, Robert S. *Martin Delany, Frederick Douglass, and the politics of representative identity.* Chapel Hill: University of North Carolina Press, 1997.

Lewis, David Levering. *W.E.B. Du Bois: Biography of a Race, 1868-1919.* New York: Henry Holt and Company, 1993.

Lipsitz, George. *The Possessive Investment in Whiteness: How White People Profit from Identity Politics.* Philadelphia: Temple University Press, 1998.

Lubiano, Wahneema, ed. *The House That Race Built.* New York: Vintage Books, 1998.

Magubane, Bernard Makhosezwe. *The Ties That Bind: African-American Consciousness of Africa.* Trenton, NJ: Africa World Press, 1987.

Marx, Jo Ann. "Myth and Meaning in Martin Delany's *Blake; or, The Huts of America.*" *College Language Association Journal.* 38.2 (1994): 183-92.

Matthews, Victoria Earle. "The Value of Race Literature: An Address Delivered at the First Congress of Colored Women of the United States." 1895. *With Pen and Voice: A Critical Anthology of Nineteenth-Century African American Women.* Ed. Shirley Wilson Logan. Carbondale: Southern Illinois University Press, 1995.

McAdoo, Bill. *Pre-Civil War Black Nationalism.* New York: The David Walker Press, 1983.

McKay, Nellie Y. Introduction. *The Unruly Voice: Rediscovering Pauline Hopkins.* Ed. John Cullen Gruesser. Urbana, IL: University of Chicago Press, 1996.

—. "The Souls of Black Women Folk in the Writings of W.E.B. DuBois." *Reading Black, Reading Feminist: A Critical Anthology.* Ed. Henry Louis Gates, Jr. New York: Meridian, 1990.

Miller, Floyd J. Introduction. *Blake; or, The Huts of America.* By Martin Delany. Boston: Beacon Press, 1970.

Minogue, Kenneth R. *Nationalism.* New York: Basic Books, 1967.

Morrison, Toni. "Home." *The House That Race Built.* Ed. Wahneema Lubiano. New York: Vintage Books, 1998.

Moses, Wilson Jeremiah. *Black Messiahs and Uncle Toms: Social and Literary Manipulations of a Religious Myth.* University Park, PA: The Penn State University Press, 1982.

—. *The Golden Age of Black Nationalism, 1850-1925.* New York: Oxford University Press, 1988.

—. Introduction. *Classic Black Nationalism.* New York: New York University Press, 1978. 1-42.

——. "Literary Garveyism: The Novels of Reverend Sutton E. Griggs." *Phylon* 40 (1979): 203-16.

——. Ed. *Liberian Dreams: Back to Africa Narratives from the 1850s*. University Park, PA: Pennsylvania State UP, 1998.

——. "The Poetics of Ethiopianism: W.E.B. DuBois and Literary Black Nationalism." *American Literature* 47:3(Nov 1975).

——. *The Wings of Ethiopia: Studies in African-American Life and Letters*. Ames: Iowa State University Press, 1990.

Nearing, Scott. *The Tragedy of Empire*. New York: Island Press, 1945.

Omi, Michael and Howard Winant. *Racial Formation in the United States*. New York: Routledge, 1986.

Otten, Thomas J. "Pauline Hopkins and the Hidden Self of Race." *ELH 59* (1992) 227-256.

Painter, Nell Irvin. *Exodusters: Black Migration to Kansas after Reconstruction*. New York: Alfred A. Knopf, 1977.

Pease, William H. and Jane Pease. *Black Utopia: Negro Communal Experiments in America*. Madison: The State Historical Society of Wisconsin, 1963.

Peterson, Carla L. *"Doers of the Word": African American Women Speakers and Writers in the North (1830-1880)*. New York: Oxford University Press, 1995.

——. "Capitalism, Black (Under)development, and the Production of the African-American Novel in the 1850s." *American Literary History*. 4 (Winter 1992): 559-83.

Pfaff, William. *The Wrath of Nation: Civilization and the Furies of Nationalism*. New York: Simon and Schuster, 1993.

Pinkney, Alphonso. *Red, Black, and Green: Black Nationalism in the United States*. Cambridge: Cambridge University Press, 1976.

Pryse, Majorie and Hortense Spillers. *Conjuring: Black Women, Fiction and Literary Tradition.* Bloomington, IN: Indiana University Press, 1990.

Rahming, Melvin B. *The Evolution of the West Indian's Image in the Afro-American Novel.* Millwood, NY: Associated Faculty Press, Inc., 1986.

Rampersad, Arnold. *The Art and Imagination of W.E.B. Du Bois.* 1976. New York: Schocken Books, 1990.

Renan, Ernest. "What is a Nation?" *Nation and Narration.* Ed. Homi K. Bhabha. New York: Routledge, 1990.

Rideout, Walter B. *The Radical Novel in the United States.* Cambridge, MA: Harvard University Press, 1956.

Roediger, David R. *The Wages of Whiteness.* New York: Verso, 1999

Rollin, Frank A. *Life and Public Services of Martin R. Delany.* New York: Arno Press, 1969.

Saxton, Alexander. *The Rise and Fall of the White Republic: Class Politics and Mass Culture in Nineteenth Century America.* New York: Verso, 1997.

Schraufnagel, Noel. *From Apology to Protest: The Black American Novel.* Deland, FL: Everett/Edwards, 1973.

Schuyler, George S. "Negro-Art Hokum." *Within The Circle: An Anthology of African American Literary Criticism from the Harlem Renaissance to the Present.* Ed. Angleyn Mitchell. Durham, NC: Duke University Press, 1994.

Seton-Watson, Hugh. *Nations and States.* Boulder, CO: Westview Press, 1977.

Singh, Amritjit. *The Novels of the Harlem Renaissance: twelve Black Writers, 1923-1933.* University Park, PA: The Penn State University Press, 1976.

Spenser, Benjamin T. *The Quest for Nationality: An American Literary Campaign.* Syracuse, NY: Syracuse University Press, 1957.

Stalin, Joseph. *Marxism and the National Question.* Moscow: Foreign Languages Publishing House, 1954.

Stepto, Robert B. *From Behind the Veil: A Study of Afro-American Narrative.* Urbana: University of Illinois Press, 1979.

Sterling, Dorothy. *The Making of an Afro-American: Martin Robinson Delany, African Explorer, Civil War Major, and Father of Black Nationalism.* New York: DA Capo Press, 1996.

Stuckey, Sterling. *Going Through the Storm: The Influence of African American Art in History.* New York: Oxford University Press, 1994.

— . *Slave Culture: Nationalist Theory and the Foundations of Black America.* New York: Oxford University Press, 1987.

Sundquist, Eric J. *To Wake the Nations: Race in the Making of American Literature.* Cambridge: Harvard University Press, 1993.

Takaki, Ronald T. *Violence in the Black Imagination.* New York: Putnam, 1972.

Tate, Claudia. "Pauline Hopkins: Our Literary Foremother." *Conjuring. Eds.* Marjorie Pryse and Hortense J. Spillers. Bloomington, Indiana: Indiana University Press, 1985.

— . *Psychoanalysis and Black Novels: Desire and the Protocols of Race.* New York: Oxford UP, 1998.

Ullman, Victor. Martin R. Delany: *The Beginnings of Black Nationalism.* Boston: Beacon Press, 1971.

Walker, David. *Walker's Appeal, with a Brief Sketch of His Life.* (New York: J.H. Tobitt, 1848). Nashville, Tennessee: James C. Winston Publishing Company, Inc., 1994.

Wallace, Maurice. "'Are We Men?': Prince Hall, Martin Delany, and the Masculine Ideal in Black Freemasonry, 1775-1865." *American Literary History* 9.2 (1997): 397-423.

Works Cited

— . *Constructing the Black Masculine: Identity and Ideality in African American Men's Literature and Culture, 1775-1995.* Durham, NC: Duke UP, 2002.

Watt, Ian P. *The Rise of the Novel: Studies in Defoe, Richardson, and Fielding.* Berkeley: University of California Press, 1964.

Weisbord, Robert G. *Ebony Kinship: African, Africans, and the Afro-American.* Westport, CT: Greenwood Press, Inc., 1973.

Welter, Barbara. *Dimity Convictions: The American Woman in the Nineteenth Century.* Athens: Ohio University Press, 1976.

Williams, Richard. *Hierarchical Structures and Social Values: The Creation of Black and Irish Identities in the United States.* Cambridge University Press, 1990

Winston, Henry. *Strategy for a Black Agenda: A Critique of New Theories of Liberation in the United States.* New York: International Publishers, 1973.

Wortham, Anne. *The Other Side of Racism: A Philosophical Study of Black Race Consciousness.* Ohio: Ohio State University Press, 1981.

Yarborough, Richard Alan. "The Depiction of Blacks in the Early Afro-American Novel." Ph.D. Dissertation, Stanford University, 1980.

Yellin, Jean Fagan. *The Intricate Knot: Black Figures in American Literature, 1776-1863.* New York: New York University Press, 1972.

INDEX

African Americans

    assumed societal inclusion, 86-87

    attitudes, 55, 126-27, 157

        associated with racial exclusion, 149

        towards blackness, 87-91

    disempowement of, 94-95, 141

    duality of psyche, 53

    education, 55-59

    hindrances in social uplift, 62

    humanity of, 26

    leadership and religion in, 125, 127

    partial racial inclusion of, 64

    political exclusion and literary stereotyping, 31

    in politics, 142-43

    post-reconstruction social life, 51-52

    pursuit towards societal inclusion, 68-69, 92, 101, 146

    spirituality, 96-97, 105, 146-147, 152-155

    unity, 56

Anglo-Saxon resistance, 98

Antebellum America, 32, 49

Assimilation, 51

Autobiography of an Ex-Coloured Man, The, African American consciousness in, 108-9

B

Black empowerment, political strategies for, 30

Black home and family, 36

Black leadership, 65, 75

Sundquist, Eric, 30
        views on *Dark Princess*, 132

T
Telassar, 97-101

U
Uncle Tom's Cabin, 27
Unsullied womanhood, 35-36

W
Walker, David, 84
Washington, Booker T., arguments related to legal rights, 69
White Christianity, criticism of, 67
Whites. *See also* Blacks
        attitudes towards African American women, 61-63
        interpretation of Africa, 69
        supremacy of, 156

About the Author

Adenike Marie Davidson is a native New Yorker and an Associate Professor of English at Fisk University. She is the author of articles published in *College Language Association Journal* and *The Southern Quartlerly*. Her research areas include Black womanhood and feminist theory, Black nationalism and reclaiming nineteenth century African American literary texts.